PRAISE FOR *INFLUENCE REDEFINED*

"Stacey Hanke's thought-provoking book is changing the way people think about influence. *Influence Redefined* reveals the truth about influence—that it is not an innate talent but rather a learned skill and that leaders are influential by design rather than by accident. Clearly, influence is changing, and we as leaders need to change as well."

—DON YAEGER, Nine-time *New York Times* best-selling
author and contributing writer for *Success* magazine

"Want greater impact and influence? YOU NEED THIS BOOK! Kudos to Hanke for writing a relevant, actionable guide that reveals the little things that make the biggest difference in influencing others."

—DAVID HORSAGER, CEO, Trust Edge Leadership
Institute and national best-selling author

"I continue to be awed and inspired by Stacey Hanke and her ability to deliver clear, concise, easy-to-activate guidance to people every day. What makes her stand out is her honest, real, and authentic approach. She truly walks it, talks it, breathes it, owns it. Many people claim to be the expert . . . Stacey just is."

—ALISA FISER, Vice President, Human Resources,
Coca-Cola Refreshments

"In *Influence Redefined*, Stacey Hanke masterfully shows how effective communication is not only a lost art, but also the true secret to influencing others. Her message is critical for those looking to develop their skills as a leader, presenter, or sales professional."

—PHILIP L. HILDEBRANDT, CFA, Chief Executive
Officer, Segall Bryant & Hamill

"*Influence Redefined* will be a wake-up call for many leaders. It definitely hit a nerve with me. Dare I say it is a scary read because it acts as a mirror into what you are doing right and what needs to be improved in real time. Keep this book within arm's reach at all times, refer to it often, and it will become your lighthouse for true leadership."

—MARK LEBLANC, Author of *Never Be the Same* and *Growing Your Business*

"Stacey Hanke has a deep understanding of what it takes to be distinctively influential in the modern-day workplace. Relevant and tangible, the methods she shares in *Influence Redefined* will help you examine your ability to communicate and ultimately improve the impact you have on your organization."

—TIM LAWRENCE, Global Lean Six Sigma Black Belt and global animal-health manufacturer

"Stacey Hanke makes it refreshingly clear that influence isn't something that can just be turned on and off, but rather is the outcome of an everyday commitment to communicate with care, passion, authenticity, and thoughtful preparation. Her insights and recommendations ring true. Embracing and acting upon them will put any professional well along the path to living and communicating in a more rewarding, influential manner."

—BOB RAIDT, Chief Executive Officer, Arc Worldwide

"*Influence Redefined* addresses a subject that is vitally important but not given nearly enough attention—the connection between communication and influence. If you're not communicating with influence, people aren't listening to you. The cost is huge, both personally and professionally. Leaders who want to elevate their executive presence and enhance their influence will benefit greatly from this book."

—TOM BELL, President and CEO, Kansas Hospital Association

"From the moment we are born, most of us wonder how we can impact this world. We hope to be inspiring. We hope to leave our permanent mark. The question is, how? The answer, my friends, is through greater influence. In her new book, *Influence Redefined*, Stacey Hanke tells us everything we need to know to be truly influential. She challenges us to go above and beyond with her step-by-step method and provides fascinating insights into how respected leaders influence others. I encourage you to accept Stacey's challenge to become your most influential self."

—SIMON T. BAILEY, Hall of Fame speaker
and author of *Shift Your Brilliance*

"In a time when executives often think they can flip a switch and turn influence on, Stacey Hanke's work is ground breaking. As she brilliantly points out, influence is a day-by-day, minute-by-minute challenge. It is a way to think, to drive action, and to be on a daily basis. It is a way of being that transcends every aspect of a person's life, not just his or her career. *Influence Redefined* will have a long-lasting impact in tangible and intangible ways and help you get whatever you want more of in your work or life."

—STEVE RICHMAN, President, Milwaukee Tool

YOU MAY NOT BE AS INFLUENTIAL

AS YOU THINK YOU ARE . . .

Other Books by Stacey Hanke

*Yes You Can! Everything You Need From A to Z to
Influence Others to Take Action*

BE THE LEADER
YOU WERE MEANT TO BE,
Monday to Monday®

INFLUENCE
REDEFINED

STACEY HANKE

GREENLEAF
BOOK GROUP PRESS

Published by Greenleaf Book Group Press
Austin, Texas
www.gbgpress.com

Copyright ©2017 Stacey Hanke Inc

Distributed by Greenleaf Book Group

For ordering information or special discounts for bulk purchases, please contact Greenleaf Book Group at PO Box 91869, Austin, TX 78709, 512.891.6100.

Design and composition by Greenleaf Book Group
Cover design by Greenleaf Book Group

Developmental Editor & Contributing Writer: Juli Baldwin, The Baldwin Group, Dallas, TX, Juli@BaldwinGrp.com

"Monday to Monday" is a propriety service mark of Stacey Hanke Inc.
Cover image © Juergen Priewe. Used under license from Shutterstock.com

Cataloging-in-Publication data is available.

Print ISBN: 978-1-62634-357-3

eBook ISBN: 978-1-62634-358-0

Part of the Tree Neutral® program, which offsets the number of trees consumed in the production and printing of this book by taking proactive steps, such as planting trees in direct proportion to the number of trees used: www.treeneutral.com

TreeNeutral

Printed in the United States of America on acid-free paper

22 23 24 25 26 27   14 13 12 11 10 9 8

First Edition

CONTENTS

ACKNOWLEDGMENTS

Where do I begin? This book has been a work in progress for four years. Those of you who know me understand that immense thought and care is put into every product, service or offering Stacey Hanke, Inc. presents to our clients. This book is no different. There have been ups and downs, questions and doubts, and at times the temptation to throw in the towel and stop writing. What pushed me through the challenges were the incredible people in my life who constantly remind me of my knowledge, determination and the impact I have on our clients.

Thank you to the most important people in my life–my family! I am blessed every day with their love, support and guidance. I am who I am because of the values my parents taught me and because my parents are amazing role models, showing me what it takes to be successful personally and professionally. I will forever admire you both for your kind hearts, generosity and determination to be happy, all while taking care of others. You have taught me to never give up, to strive for what I'm passionate about and to be thankful for what I have. No words can express my love for you and how thankful I am to learn from both of you.

Thank you to my partner and the love of my life, Jeff. For the many times you met me at the coffee shop to read another draft of this book, for understanding the many days and nights I spend away from home impacting others across the country, for being there to welcome me home, and for expressing your love and how proud you are of me. I am truly the luckiest woman! I love you forever!

Thank you to my sisters, Crystal and Lisa, who believed in me so much that you joined me in the company. I could not run this business without you. This journey we are taking together is brighter and even more exciting with you both by my side. You inspire me to be the best I can be. Celebrating our successes is a lot more fun with you here to "high five." Here's to many more years of success!

Thank you to my brothers-in-law–my two Todds–for your constant support! Thank you as well to my nieces, Olivia, Julia, Jayla and Sienna. Your energy and appreciation of the little things in life remind me to not take life too seriously and to enjoy this wild ride. I love all of you to the moon and back!

Thank you to my friends for accepting me for who I am, including this busy career I have chosen. I am proud and honored to have amazing friends who will always be there for me no matter what. You are too many to list, but you know who you are.

Thank you to my business coach, Mark LeBlanc, who has been by my side for many, many years, through thick and thin. I never thought I would thank someone for pushing me so far outside of my comfort zone and for giving me feedback that sometimes is tough to hear. Yet it is because of your guidance and motivation that I have grown personally and professionally in a way I never imagined was possible. Thank you, Mark, for helping me discover my potential and inspiring me to go after it!

I also want to thank Lou Heckler, my long-time speech coach. It has been a privilege to work with the best of the best in the industry. Your insights and guidance have helped me better engage, captivate and connect with audiences for maximum impact. You helped me develop my authentic style and stand out from the crowd. Thank you for not only being my coach, but also a dear friend who has always had my back.

Stacey Hanke, Inc. would not exist without our outstanding team. It has taken years to build this best-in-class group of professionals, yet it has been well worth the effort. Your dedication, loyalty, drive and support are hands down beyond that of any team I have ever worked with. You serve our clients with sincere care and passion for our work as if this were your own company. We have each other's backs and not a day goes by that I am not thankful for having all of you in my corner.

Thank you to my writer, Juli Baldwin. You have stuck by me through the ups and downs, determined to help me share my experiences and knowledge with others. Your expertise and ability to capture my ideas, voice and style are impressive. You have helped me bring this book to life while encouraging me to never settle until our writing was exceptional. I am forever thankful you have stepped into my life.

Thank you to our clients for your partnership. You continue to push us to go beyond what we think is possible. We pinch ourselves every day because we know how fortunate we are to do what we love with people like you. You drive us to work harder, to never stop learning and to have fun.

A sincere thank you to you, the reader! Whether we have worked together, you participated in one of my presentations or workshops, or someone encouraged you to pick up this book, I am glad you are here. My goal in writing this book was to help you become the leader you were meant to be, Monday to Monday®. The personal stories and experiences come from the heart to show you that if I can grow my influence, you can too. I would be honored to hear how this book has benefited you and those you influence. You can reach me at stacey@staceyhankeinc.com.

Enjoy every page!

ARE YOU REALLY AS INFLUENTIAL AS YOU THINK YOU ARE?

How influential are you . . . *really?*

If you aren't consistently getting the results you want—as an individual, as a leader, as a professional—perhaps you're not as influential as you think you are. I realize that's a bold statement just a few sentences into a book. After all, I don't even know you.

But what if I'm right?

Why not stay with me for at least the first few chapters and find out?

In my experience, most leaders aren't as influential as they think they are. Michael* is a great example. I met Michael, a senior executive with a multinational firm, at one of my leadership workshops. At the end of the day, after all the other participants had left, he came up to talk to me. "Wow, you really opened my eyes today," he said.

"I have a high-powered job with a lot of responsibility," Michael explained. "I've worked hard to get where I'm at. I think of myself as confident, credible and influential, and I'm always conscious of my presence." As he shared his perception of himself, I noted that his appearance matched his demeanor. "But your session has me questioning just how influential I really am.

"Several months ago I made a presentation to a prospective client about a huge contract," he continued. "I was sure I had nailed it and that

....

* Not his real name. Minor details have been changed to protect the individual's identity.

we would win the contract. Later that day, I used one of those limo services to get to the airport. During the ride, the prospective client called to
ask a follow-up question, and we talked for several minutes.

"When I got off the phone, the driver asked if he could give me
some feedback. I thought that was kind of odd. So at first, honestly, I
just ignored him and kept looking at my phone. But then he asked again.

"When I looked up, he was staring at me in the rearview mirror.
I figured there must be something wrong with how I looked. You
know . . . lint on my suit, spot on my tie, spinach in my teeth from
lunch. I gave myself a quick once-over but didn't notice anything.

"At that point, I didn't want to be rude so I said, 'Sure, bring it on.'

"Get this . . . the driver said, 'I chauffeur a lot of high-powered executives. When you first got in the car, you looked like you were a big deal.
But then I overheard your phone conversation. It was difficult to follow
what you were saying, and it took you a long time to get to the point.
And you say *um* and *uh* a lot. I mean no disrespect, sir, but I thought
you would want to know.'"

(You may be thinking, like I was, there is no way this story actually
happened. I have heard a lot of crazy stories from leaders over the years,
but this one seemed outlandish. What limousine driver says something
like that to a passenger, especially an executive? I politely questioned
Michael about the incident, and he assured me it was true. That limo
driver must have had incredible moxie or been looking for a reason to
get fired. I guess sometimes the truth really is stranger than fiction.)

As Michael continued to tell me his story, his expression became
quite animated. "Well, as you can imagine, I was ticked off! I couldn't
believe the nerve of this guy criticizing me like that! And I was caught
off guard . . . I didn't know how to respond. No one had ever said anything like that to me before.

"Fortunately, right then we pulled up to the airport. I got out, slammed
the door and walked away. I just wrote off him and his 'feedback' as clueless and didn't give it a second thought . . . until today."

Michael paused for a moment. "During your session, you explained that most people aren't as influential as they think they are, but they don't know it partly because they rarely get honest feedback. That was when it suddenly hit me–*what if that driver was right?* The feedback he gave me is probably what everyone else is thinking but won't say to my face.

"I used to think I was fairly influential," he continued, looking dismayed. "Now I realize I'm probably not as influential as I thought."

Standing there listening to Michael, my heart went out to him. Like so many of the leaders I work with, he had inadvertently fallen into a trap of disbelief and denial. It is tough to watch individuals come to the realization that they lack true influence or have damaged what influence they did have. Yet I know from experience that self-awareness is a difficult but necessary step to growing one's influence.

Although Michael's story certainly was different than any I had heard before, the theme was one I am all too familiar with. I have had the privilege to train and coach tens of thousands of leaders across the country. These leaders represent a diverse cross-section of industries, functional areas, leadership levels (from C-suites to directors), ages and gender. Even today, I am still amazed at how differently individuals perceive their level of influence compared to reality.

The vast majority of leaders–I estimate 95 percent–**think they are more influential than they actually are.**

You may be thinking, *Wow! That number is really high! How can that be?* I'm confident in my estimate of 95 percent because of what my team and I have observed almost daily in our work with clients over many years. In our workshops, we see the profound self-awareness that occurs as individuals watch themselves on video playback for the first time. The CEOs and executives I coach one-on-one come to realize that they are not as influential as they thought they were and that it affects their ability to lead. Frequently after my keynotes, people come forward to tell me they now understand that they have to grow their influence.

Why is it so common for people to overestimate their level of influence? First is the phenomenon called Illusory Superiority or the Above Average Effect, one of the cornerstones of social and personal psychology.[1] Most people consistently judge themselves better than average in any particular metric, including personality traits, job performance and work-related skills. We overestimate our positive qualities and underestimate our negative qualities.

The second reason leaders believe they are more influential than they really are is because our definition of influence is flawed. **We have a misperception of what influence is and an outdated, inadequate understanding of what it means to be influential.**

> *Most of us believe we are more influential than we actually are.*

The common definition of influence is the ability to motivate people to take action. While that is certainly true, it's not the complete picture—not by a long shot. This definition is vague and limited. It's vague because it is neither precise nor bottom-line oriented and therefore not meaningful. It's limited because there are other elements of influence that need to be taken into account. For example, much of the current thinking about influence glosses over or altogether misses a key component of influence: communication.

The current influence paradigm simply doesn't work in today's business environment. It is all about status quo, and status quo doesn't cut it in a global, highly competitive marketplace. The current way of thinking about influence also doesn't contemplate the pervasive and often undesirable impacts of technology. Here is a brutal truth: The people you are trying to influence–whether they are customers, team members or investors–*aren't paying attention to you.* If you don't have their attention, you can't influence them.

We need to change the way we think about influence.

Based on more than two decades of experience and my work with high-performance organizations in a wide array of industries, I have developed a more meaningful definition of influence. This new definition is not only specific and complete, but also relevant to today's world of business. Influence as I define it is—

- **Monday to Monday**–consistent actions all the time, in all situations, that are congruent with your purpose and priorities
- Moving people to action *long after the interaction is over*
- **Creating a standout experience** that separates you from the crowd
- **Built on verbal and nonverbal communication**
- Measured not by how you feel but by the **results you consistently achieve**
- A **skill that can be developed** by anyone through feedback, practice and accountability

We live in a soundbite world, yet not everything can be–or should be–condensed into 140 characters. Bottom line, redefining influence is about reaching your full potential, achieving consistent results and becoming the leader you were meant to be, Monday to Monday®.

If you are like many of the leaders I interact with, you have already achieved a certain level of success. You've worked hard and have ample knowledge, experience and credibility. Yet something made you curious about this book. Perhaps you have plateaued, and you've been wondering how to jump-start your career. Maybe your results have flattened out or even dropped off. If you're in sales, you might be looking for an edge over the competition. If you're a senior executive, perhaps you are looking for ways to more effectively lead your organization or to better communicate with investors or your board of directors.

You can take yourself to a higher degree of influence and achieve a level of success you might not even realize is possible. I know this to be true because I've had the joy of observing numerous leaders implement the ideas in this book to scale their influence and make an even greater impact in their organizations, their communities and their families.

You may be thinking of several people you know who could benefit from this book–colleagues, friends, coworkers—who aren't as influential as they think they are. You may also be thinking that this book doesn't pertain to you. "They" need to enhance their influence, not you. Let me ask you—

- Are your listeners often active on their electronic devices while you're talking?
- Do you fail to get discretionary effort from your team, especially when you're not present?
- Do you ever find yourself rambling in conversations?
- Do you wish more people would follow your lead?
- Are you frequently interrupted?
- Do you typically run out of time in a presentation before you've made your key points?
- Do customers not buy from you like they used to?
- Do others not respond to your emails and texts as quickly as you would like?
- Was the last time you recorded yourself (audio/video) more than thirty days ago?
- Do you wish you could consistently get the results you want?
- Are you the only one talking during a meeting?

If you answered "yes" to five or more of these questions, you may not be as influential as you think you are. If you answered yes to three of these questions, you likely are not influential Monday to Monday®. If you responded "no" to all of these questions, let me ask you this: Are you influential by design or by accident? Are you willing to leave your influence, your results and your success to chance?

Business guru Jim Collins teaches that *good* is often the enemy of *great* when it comes to building an enduring organization. The same principle holds true for individuals. Growing your influence requires that you leave *good* behind in pursuit of something more. Believing that your current level of influence is good enough to achieve the success you desire in the future is perhaps the biggest obstacle holding you back.

You won't know how much better you can be—how much more influential you can be—until you know what *better* looks like. Let's see what true influence looks like. Are you ready? Let's get started.

HOW TO GET THE MOST VALUE FROM THIS BOOK
IN THE SHORTEST TIME

Influence Redefined is about rethinking your approach to influence. It is likely different than any other information you've read or heard about influence. Most discussions about influence cover the broad concepts, but few give detailed specifics about *how* to become more influential.

My purpose with this book is to reveal what it takes to be truly influential Monday to Monday® and to share a proven, step-by-step method for how to get there. I've included practical, time-tested how-tos and action steps so you can immediately begin growing your influence. You'll also find insights and perspectives from dozens of executives, leaders and business professionals who have successfully used the concepts presented to enhance their influence. They are the proof that the principles and tools I share in this book work in the real world.

If you truly want to get the most out of this book in the shortest amount of time, you're going to have to take action beyond just reading it. While it would be great if you could simply read a book and magically be more influential, we both know that is wishful thinking, right? If you want to be more influential, you're going to have to practice the skills and techniques of influence. To help you do that, I've included a section at the end of every chapter in Parts II and III titled "Take Action." This is where you'll find tools and tips for practicing the concepts presented, as well as real-life situations where you can immediately apply them. Practice these skills in your current daily interactions, and you will begin to see results right away.

Part I

INFLUENCE REDEFINED

CHAPTER 1

IS YOUR INFLUENCE OUTDATED?

The challenge begins with the mistaken belief that how we
influenced others in the past still works in today's world of business.

Let's go back to Michael, my client who received the gift of feedback
from a car-service driver. There is more to his story.

Like I did, you may have wondered if Michael and his company got
the contract he was so confident they would win. It turns out the contract was awarded to a different company, a new player in the industry.

When I asked Michael why he thought they didn't get the business,
he said, "I felt like I gave a powerful
and persuasive presentation to the
client. And I don't think I lost the
deal because of that less-than-stellar
phone call with my contact on the
way to the airport, although it probably didn't help.

> The business environment has
> changed dramatically in recent
> years, yet our understanding of
> influence hasn't kept pace with
> changing times.

"When I followed up with my
contact, she said the company they chose didn't have a significantly
better solution, cheaper price or more experienced team," Michael
explained. "She said they just felt more confident in the other organization's ability to meet their needs."

Although he didn't realize it at first, what really happened here was that Michael and his team lacked the influence necessary to close the deal. I share Michael's story because it's a powerful example of what many leaders around the country are now discovering: **how we have defined influence in the past doesn't consistently produce results in the new world of business.** Michael and his team were playing by the old rules in a new game and still expecting to win.

While we are all aware (perhaps somewhat painfully) that the business environment has changed dramatically in recent years, few recognize that our understanding of influence hasn't kept pace with changing times:

- Too many leaders still buy into common misconceptions about how we gain influence and what it means to be influential.
- Technology has made it easier for us to communicate, yet much more difficult for us to influence others.
- *Good* is no longer good enough in a competitive global marketplace.
- In today's business world, effective leadership requires influence not only in high-stakes situations but Monday to Monday®.

The prevailing influence paradigm is out of date. The world has changed yet our concept of influence hasn't. Let's find out why.

THE THREE MYTHS OF INFLUENCE

I wish I had a dollar for every time I've heard a client say, "I'm influential when I need to be" or "I have influence because I am a [insert any number of executive titles here–CEO, VP, etc.]." If only these sentiments were true. Influence would be so much easier.

Much of our thinking (and therefore our actions) around influence is based on misconceptions and mistaken beliefs. If we want to update our thinking about influence, we first need to address what I call the Three Myths of Influence.

Myth #1: "I feel influential, therefore I am."

Many people believe that if they feel they are a certain way (such as a good driver or an effective communicator), then it must be true. All too often, leaders mistakenly believe that if they feel influential, then others perceive them the same way. This problem is compounded by the fact that few people are willing to give leaders honest feedback about their influence or lack thereof. As a result, they take their level of influence for granted.

The vice president of sales for a large organization recently told me, "I've been doing [sales presentations] a long time. I'm always comfortable. I never get nervous when I present." I quickly pointed out that comfort doesn't equal influence!

Just because you feel confident, credible and knowledgeable, and the person sitting across the table from you is nodding his or her head yes, does not mean you *are* influential. The proof is in the other person's actions. Will they do what you want them to do—buy your product or service, accept your recommendation, follow your lead?

REALITY: Influence is evidenced by results.

Myth #2: Influence is situational.

Many leaders believe influence is a skill set that can be turned on and off, used only as necessary. We show up for the big event or critical conversation and "turn it on," meaning we are very conscious of our demeanor, our presence, the words we speak, how we deliver those words, and how we interact with those around us. We turn our influence on for key presentations, sales and creative pitches, board meetings, product launch events, conferences, important meetings or when it's time to rally the team around a goal.

Outside of these high-stakes events, we tend to turn our influence off. We seem to think it's not necessary to be influential in our routine, daily interactions—answering the phone, typing out a text or chatting in the hallway. This mindset leads to inconsistent behavior and unpredictable communication between leaders and listeners.

True influence is Monday to Monday®. There is so much more to influence than showing up and giving a powerful presentation or having a meaningful conversation. Real influence is developed not through a series of one-time events, but rather through the accumulation of our daily actions and interactions.

REALITY: Influence is all the time, in every situation.

Myth #3: Title = Influence.

There is a myth in corporate America that influence comes with a title. We operate under the assumption that the higher our position, the longer we have been in our field or industry, or the bigger our success, the greater our influence by default. Many leaders confuse authority and power with the ability to have impact and influence on those around them. You may have power, but do people follow you? Do they willingly act on what you have to say?

The truth is that position and influence are not directly correlated. An impressive title doesn't buy you a pass. Influence is not a badge of honor you receive as you move up the corporate ladder. It's not determined by years of service, pay grade, or even contribution or value to an organization.

We inherently know this myth isn't true when we observe other executives or high-level leaders who lack influence. Yet we don't consider that same possibility might be true for ourselves. The further irony of this myth is that as you are promoted, your need for influence increases, but a bigger salary and corner office don't guarantee you will have greater influence. Those with powerful titles are expected to be influential leaders, yet many aren't.

In *The 21 Irrefutable Laws of Leadership*, John Maxwell states, "True leadership cannot be awarded, appointed or assigned. It comes only from influence, and that cannot be mandated. It must be earned. The only thing a title can buy is a little time–either to increase your level of influence with others or to undermine it."[2]

"An individual's title doesn't predict influence, which is a problem, especially for someone in my position," the CEO of an international advertising agency once said to me. "I often wonder, are people telling me what they think I want to hear because I'm the CEO? Or am I influential because people genuinely believe I have good ideas?" The good news for this executive is that he truly is influential.

REALITY: Anyone has the capacity to be influential if they are willing to do the work.

Myths and misconceptions are just a few of the many factors that undermine influence. As long as we hang on to these outdated beliefs, we limit our potential to enhance our influence. Do you subscribe to any of the Three Myths of Influence?

The Top Ten Lies We Tell Ourselves about Our Influence

1. I'm an executive/leader–I'm already influential.
2. I can turn on influence when I need to.
3. I feel confident, credible and knowledgeable, so others must experience me the same way.
4. Influence only occurs in face-to-face situations.
5. Having influence in day-to-day interactions isn't necessary or important.
6. People are on their phones while I talk because that is just today's culture.
7. My work sells itself. I don't have to be influential.
8. What I've done in the past has gotten me where I am, and it's good enough to get me where I want to go in the future.
9. Influence is a "soft skill" that doesn't really matter in the digital age.
10. I'm comfortable in high-stakes situations, and if I'm comfortable I must be influential.

TECHNOLOGY: THE DOUBLE-EDGED SWORD

I recently attended a conference where I presented on the topic of influence. On the day of my arrival, I had trouble finding the exact conference location, and I texted the conference coordinator asking for specific directions. Her responses were abrupt and harsh, almost bordering on rude. When I met her in person, I found her to be the complete opposite: approachable, pleasant and welcoming. I presumed the tone of her earlier texts was simply due to stress.

When she and I emailed after the conference, her responses were again curt. I was surprised that someone in such a visible position wasn't more aware of her virtual persona. If I had never met this woman in person, my perception of her would be based solely on how she came across in her emails and texts. This experience made me wonder how many people have a less-than-positive perception of her and how that might be negatively impacting her business.

Technology has affected almost every aspect of our professional and personal lives, including our ability to influence others. With respect to influence, technology is a double-edged sword. **Technology has made it easier for us to communicate, yet much more difficult for us to influence others Monday to Monday®.**

In an always-on, always-connected world, we tend to overlook the importance of influence. Too often, we don't stop to think about how we show up or how our communication will be received. Case in point: the message at the bottom of emails sent via smart phones asking recipients for forgiveness of our spelling errors. It's easier and faster—yet far less influential—to ask forgiveness than to check ourselves before we hit send.

Recent statistics indicate that eighty-nine billion business emails are sent worldwide each day.[3] According to The Radicati Group, the average corporate email user sends and receives between 105 and 125 email messages per day.[4] That is an astounding number that doesn't even include text messages. A report by Heywire Business found that 67 percent of business professionals use text messaging for business-related communication. Of those professionals, 72 percent text with internal coworkers and 51 percent text with external contacts such as customers, prospects and vendors. Furthermore, more than 33 percent of sales professionals say they have closed a business deal via text. The report concluded, "Business has stopped talking and started texting."[5]

Have you ever thought about how many emails and texts you send each day? Have you thought about how each of those messages impacts your influence? Each one is an opportunity to stand out from the crowd and grow your influence. Each one is also an opportunity to be misinterpreted, to damage your reputation and to negate your influence. Welcome to the new world of business, where your influence is always on display.

Your influence is always on display.

When it comes to influence, every interaction matters.

If you remember nothing else from this book, remember this one point: Every single interaction—even the virtual ones—matters. Every presentation, conversation, impromptu meeting, email, text, picture, video, post or phone call in the back of a taxi—is a representation of who you are and directly determines how others experience you. Every interaction is a representation of your voice and your personal brand and establishes your reputation. Every interaction either enhances or detracts from your influence.

YOU CAN'T INFLUENCE THEM IF THEY AREN'T PAYING ATTENTION

Imagine that you've been preparing for a critical meeting for several weeks. You've done your research and dissected your slides ten times. You've even practiced your presentation. As you walk confidently to the front of the room to deliver your presentation, you look out over the group and what do you see? A room full of people on their electronic devices, heads bowed in the "smartphone prayer."

Now this might not be a problem if everyone disconnects and turns off their devices when the meeting starts. Wishful thinking! How often does that happen? They will silence their devices when you ask them to, but they will still be connected . . . and distracted.

Heywire Business reports that 97 percent of text messages are read within three minutes of delivery.[6] This suggests that the people in your audience will likely check their devices at least once, if not multiple times, during your presentation. Heywire Business also found that 59 percent of people use their personal mobile device frequently for business communications. Consequently, your listeners will not only be receiving emails and texts from customers, colleagues and team members, but also from their significant other, kids, friends and, perhaps, Amazon, confirming their order has shipped. How many of those incoming messages will result in multiple-message conversations? Probably most of them. The interruptions and distractions will be never-ending.

When you deliver that critical presentation you've worked so hard on, will you have your listeners' full attention? What is the likelihood they will all act on your recommendations? What are the chances they will even remember your message a week from now? Slim at best if you're not consistently influential.

Good news . . . you're not alone. Who hasn't found themselves in a situation where their listeners aren't fully paying attention? Most of us have also been on the other side of this example too. Have you ever sat in a meeting and found your mind wandering to weekend plans? Are you guilty of checking your email or surfing the web while on a phone call? Have you ever been in the midst of a face-to-face conversation when you hear the familiar sound of an incoming text message and wondered who it's from and what it's about?

We've all done it, and therein lies the challenge: **Every day we are trying to influence always-connected, digitally-distracted, often-over-scheduled, multitasking individuals.**

The digital age has generated a staggering amount of digital noise. It is pervasive, constant and deafening. Digital distractions make it exponentially more difficult to capture and keep your listeners' and readers' attention. This is one of the key reasons why typical influence principles don't produce results in today's business environment.

I recently heard a story about an executive who explained that he texts during meetings because, of course, it would be inappropriate to make phone calls during meetings.

At first I thought, "Seriously?" Then I realized that this story beautifully illustrates how invasive and intrusive technology has become. The new world of business is all access, all the time. Communicating via text, email and social media anywhere and anytime has become not only acceptable but the norm. As acceptable as it may be, it constantly diminishes the impact of your message and your ability to influence people to action.

Perhaps you're thinking, "Stacey, it's really not a big deal. I can quickly answer a text or email and listen to someone at the same time." You might want to reconsider that notion. While most individuals believe they can multitask, science is proving that effective multitasking is a fallacy. (A participant in one of my sessions chuckled when I shared this information with his group. "My wife will be relieved to hear this," he said. "She thinks I'm abnormal because I can't multitask.")

In a report for National Public Radio, Earl Miller, professor of neuroscience at Massachusetts Institute of Technology, explains that our brains can't focus on more than one thing at a time. Rather than truly multitasking, our brains are actually switching between tasks.

If you don't have people's attention, you can't influence them.

"Switching from task to task, you think you're actually paying attention to everything around you at the same time, but you're actually not," Miller said. Referring to an example of writing an email while talking on the phone, he said, "Those things are nearly impossible to do at the same time. You cannot focus on one while doing the other. . . . They both involve communicating via speech or the written word, and so there's a lot of conflict between the two of them."[7] The reality is that we cannot do two things at once, or at least not do them both well.

You can try to eliminate digital noise by banning all electronic devices. (Good luck with that one!) You will never be able to remove all distractions. One of the biggest obstacles to influence is something you can neither see or hear—the thoughts that are constantly playing in your listeners' and readers' heads. The report that has to be done by 5:00, the ongoing conflict with a coworker, how to get to the kid's game on time, where to go for lunch. Internal chatter is yet another distraction that drowns out you and your message.

The bottom line is this: If you don't have people's attention, you can't influence them.

In the battle for your listeners' and readers' attention, only one thing is going to win. Will it be you and your message, or their constantly chirping devices? If you are not more engaging and compelling than the digital distraction of the moment, you and your message will lose every time.

GOOD IS NO LONGER GOOD ENOUGH

"We are well-known in our industry for having top-notch products and solid relationships with our customers."

This is the message I repeatedly hear from prospective clients. These executives believe that their organizations are on the right track . . . that is, until they lose some major customers. That is usually when they contact me looking for help.

Like my client Michael and his organization in the earlier story, these organizations are typically quite competitive in terms of products, services, price and people. There is something else going on that is causing them to lose business: They lack influence with their customers. As a result, their customers don't hesitate to make a change when something better comes along. Of course, having influence doesn't guarantee that your company won't ever lose customers, but often they will at least give you the opportunity to try to keep their business.

It wasn't all that long ago that good products, good service and good people set you apart from the competition. Today, good is the minimum standard. It's not enough anymore to have high quality products and services at a competitive price, or even strong customer relationships. These factors alone won't influence people to buy in a marketplace characterized by intense competition, limited time and higher expectations. Is it possible that being *good enough* might be sabotaging your future success?

When all else is equal between you and the competition, the business goes to the one with more influence.

When all other factors are essentially the same, the sale goes to the company that customers trust the most. I do a lot of work with companies in the advertising industry, coaching them on how to create a stand-out experience with their customers. The partners of these advertising agencies tell me, "Our competitors have accountant representatives who are just as experienced as our account reps and creative people who are just as brilliant as ours. The truth is we all do similar work. Our clients tell us the reason we win the business is because we make them feel good. They trust that we are going to make the deadline and meet the budget."

It is the experience your organization and your team create for customers that influences them to buy your products and services. Zig Ziglar once said, "If people like you, they'll listen to you. If they trust you, they'll do business with you." Customers want to do business with organizations and people who are consistent, credible, trustworthy, knowledgeable, professional and passionate. It's no coincidence that these are the foundational characteristics of true influence.

When all else is equal between you and the competition, the business goes to the one with more influence.

LEADERSHIP REQUIRES INFLUENCE

Just as *good* is no longer enough to keep a profitable bottom line, being a *good* leader will no longer get you where you want to go in your career. In today's work environment, getting people to buy into your vision, act on your recommendations and follow your lead is more challenging than ever. **The new world of business requires influential leaders.**

According to Gallup's most recent *State of the Global Workplace* report, 63 percent of employees worldwide are not engaged and 24 percent are actively disengaged.[8] That means a staggering 87 percent of team members are likely unmotivated and unwilling to give more than the bare minimum required to get the job done. Now add to that the complexity of a highly diverse workforce, flatter organizational structures, virtual workplaces and the ever-present pressure to "do more with less."

Your team is only as strong as your ability to influence them. "As a leader, you can't do anything on your own," Kristin Derwinski, Director of Organizational Development at Briggs & Stratton, pointed out. "If you can't influence others to get where you want to go, you become an ineffective leader. Influence is about getting people to rally around a common cause."

A key element of effective leadership is the ability to delegate, and delegating is simply influencing others to do what you want them to do when you want them to do it. Your level of influence affects your team's morale, attitudes, culture, behavior and especially their productivity. Their results are a direct reflection of your influence as a leader.

"People have a deep desire to follow a leader who inspires them to be their best," says Mark LeBlanc, author of *Growing Your Business* and my business coach. "If a leader is influential, he or she has a greater likelihood of getting people to move mountains. The absence of influence determines whether an employee will go the extra mile or stop short of reaching his or her potential."

Lisa Zarick is Executive Vice President of Global Talent Management for Edelman (and a client of mine when she was with Leo

Burnett Worldwide). When I asked Lisa how important influence is to her job as a leader, she said, "Influence is the number one skill I use. I call upon it every day, whether I'm working with the executive team or others in the organization."

Influence for influence's sake is not the goal. In today's business environment, influence is the highest form of competitive advantage for both individuals and organizations. It is the "X factor" that trumps all else. If you have influence, customers keep coming back even when you don't have the best price. If you have influence, people keep following your lead even when you're not there.

Some people might argue that influence is irrelevant in today's business world. Nothing could be further from the truth. Influence is more crucial to success than ever. Is it possible your thinking about influence might be outdated? Maybe it's time for an influence upgrade to "Influence 2.0." In the next chapter, you'll discover how redefining influence produces real and lasting results.

Influence Monday to Monday® is the highest form of competitive advantage for both organizations and individuals.

SUMMARY

- Our current thinking about influence doesn't produce results in today's business environment.

- True influence is Monday to Monday®, evidenced by results and available to anyone willing to do the work.

- Technology has made it easier for us to communicate, yet much more difficult for us to influence others Monday to Monday®.

- Every interaction is an opportunity to enhance (or minimize) your influence.

- If you don't have people's attention, you can't influence them. You and your message must be more compelling than the digital noise constantly distracting your listeners and readers.

- When all else is equal between you and the competition, the business goes to the one with more influence.

- Influence Monday to Monday® is the highest form of competitive advantage for both organizations and individuals.

YOU MAY NOT BE AS INFLUENTIAL AS YOU THINK YOU ARE IF . . .
Your listeners are active on their electronic devices while you are talking.

Do you find yourself competing with technical gadgets? When you and your message are not interesting or when you're not directly connecting with your audience, you in effect give your listeners permission to check their devices. If people are texting, checking email or otherwise involved with their electronic devices while you're talking, it's a sure sign that they are disengaged. If your listeners aren't engaged, they won't hear your message; and if they don't hear your message, the chances of you influencing them to take action are slim—

Your natural response to this situation might be to—

- Ignore the behavior, assuming it is part of the culture
- Talk faster and louder, hoping the change will draw listeners' attention back to you (yet in reality causing them to become even more disengaged)
- Call out the offenders, making everyone feel like they are back in grade school

For Influence Monday to Monday®:

1. **Pause.** The silence will grab the offenders' attention and bring it back to you and your message.
2. **Look individuals in the eye.** When speaking, look directly at an individual for a complete sentence or thought, something most presenters don't do. Your audience will immediately sense that you are connecting with them. They also will be less likely to get sucked into their technical gadgets when they know you will catch them not paying attention.
3. **Take control.** State at the beginning with confidence, "In order to honor everyone's time and receive the value you expect from our time together, please close and silence your phones, tablets and laptops. This will also allow us to end on time."
4. **Be interesting.** Boring communicators don't grab and keep the attention of their listeners. Listeners zone out when you read from your slides, especially when they are filled to capacity with charts, graphs and unreadable fonts. No one wants to be read to. Make a real connection with your listeners by communicating with passion and authenticity.

CHAPTER 2

INFLUENCE 2.0

We need a new kind of influence for the new world of business.

When you think of someone influential, who comes to mind?

I think of Darren Hardy, publisher and founding editor of *Success* magazine.

Darren has scaled his influence to an astounding level. Before founding *Success*, he led two personal development–based television networks and launched more than one thousand programs, products and live events. The degree of influence he has achieved is evidenced by his enormous following and the caliber of people he interacts with. Darren has gained an audience with leading experts on human performance and achievement as well as innovative entrepreneurs, superstar athletes and elite entertainers. In addition, he personally mentors some of the world's top CEOs and high-performance individuals.

I've been following Darren and his work for many years. His image, brand, messaging and communication are consistent no matter the medium, whether it is one of his books, an email, tweet, video or live speech. His passion, authenticity and sincerity come through in everything he does.

As a subscriber to his daily mentoring messages, I receive an email every weekday at 6:00 a.m. in which he shares ideas to help his readers be successful that day. When Darren makes a recommendation, he also gives specific examples of how he applies the concept in his life. He openly shares his weaknesses, mistakes and how he sometimes struggles to be his best. If he makes a commitment to his readers (e.g., to send a link or share action steps), he never fails to follow up.

Darren lives by example, Monday to Monday®. As a result, he has built trust and developed influence with his followers. You just can't help but feel that you are in good hands when following his advice. His messages leave a lasting impression on me, far beyond those moments each morning when I read them. I often recall and apply one of his suggestions weeks or months later. I know Darren has had a positive impact on my life, and I suspect that is the case for many others.

Based on my experiences with him, Darren epitomizes our new definition of influence:

- Monday to Monday®–consistent all the time, in all situations
- Moves people to action long after the interaction is over
- Creates a standout experience for readers and listeners
- Built on communication
- Measured by results
- A skill that can be developed if you are willing to do the work.

This is the kind of influence you need to cultivate in order to be successful in today's business environment. If you want others to follow your lead and act on what you have to say, it may be time to update your influence.

INFLUENCE MONDAY TO MONDAY®

Have you ever been on a diet or exercise plan? Did you reach the level of health and well-being you wanted to achieve? If so, you were probably very consistent with your efforts. If you fell short of your goals, it could be because you ate well and exercised some days, but missed many others. As I am constantly reminding myself, we can't eat well or work out Monday through Friday and then blow it over the weekend if we really want to be healthy. For consistent, permanent results, we have to be all-in, all the time.

True influence works the same way. As I said earlier, influence is not something you turn on when the situation calls for it. Even being influential Monday through Friday, 8:00 a.m. to 5:00 p.m., isn't enough in today's business environment. You have to be consistently influential Monday to Monday®. This is especially true if you answer any emails, text messages and phone calls after hours and on weekends. (And who doesn't?) Being influential needs to be your default modus operandi. It should be who you are and what you do 24/7.

Consistency is a key element of influence. Inconsistency leads to a lack of trust. If people don't trust you, they won't act on your recommendations or follow your lead. I once observed a senior executive at an annual sales conference speak to his sales leaders about upcoming compensation changes. He shared his excitement for this change and how it would positively impact the sales teams in the field. During a break, one of the sales leaders overheard the executive talking to another executive. "Who knows what's going to happen with these compensation changes?" he said with a concerned look on his face.

This lack of consistency in the executive's message immediately raised a red flag with the sales leader, who went and shared what he had heard with his peers. By the time the conference reconvened, the dynamics in the room had completely changed. The sales leaders began to pepper the executive with questions: "Are our jobs at risk?" "Are we going to be asked to cut staff?" "How will this impact our customers?"

Not only did the executive's inconsistent communication create uncertainty among his sales leaders, it also damaged his credibility and reputation. His team lost trust in him, which affected his ability to lead and influence them in the future.

Have you ever experienced a situation similar to this? Do you remember how you felt and what you thought when someone said one thing in a meeting and then said something different afterward in the halls? Did your trust in them waver? Did that person have influence with you anymore?

Good leaders show up and are influential in the moment. **Influential leaders show up for every moment.** You can't discount the importance of a 140-character tweet, a quick after-hours text to a client or the description on your profile or corporate website. When your message, actions and presence are consistent, your influence grows. Consistency means that no matter whom you communicate with, what medium you communicate through or when you interact with someone, you are always seen as confident, credible and trustworthy. Someone who follows you on social media has the same experience as they do talking with you one-on-one.

Are you consistently influential Monday to Monday®? Do you bring your *A-game* to all your interactions? If you want to be perceived as an influential leader, you can't facilitate a meeting with a powerful executive presence and then follow up with an email filled with typos and mistakes (even if you send it via your phone).

Influential leaders show up for every moment.

To take your career to the next level, you have to be influential Monday to Monday®. Imagine the reputation you would create for yourself and the level of influence you would have if you put the same amount of effort, focus and preparation into every interaction. There are very few people who consistently communicate with influence. If you can train yourself to do it, you will set yourself apart from the crowd.

INFLUENCE BEYOND THE INTERACTION

Imagine that you are at a restaurant with a friend enjoying delicious food and engaging conversation. At the table next to you is a family with one parent and two children, about six and eight years old. Consider the following scenarios:

1. The children are out of their seats, running around the table and arguing loudly with each other, all while the parent sits idly by. I know you've experienced this scenario before! The parent lacks influence (and authority) with the children.

2. The children are reasonably well behaved . . . that is until the parent leaves the table for a moment, at which point they start poking each other and arguing. In this case, the parent has limited influence—the children behave appropriately as long as the parent is present.

3. The children are well behaved even when the parent leaves the table to go to the restroom. The children don't get out of their seats, flick food at each other or start an argument. Their actions and behaviors are the same whether the parent is present or not. This parent has true, Monday to Monday® influence with the children.

This example mirrors what we see in the business world. Some leaders, like some parents, have minimal influence. You can easily pick them out. Their employees often "do their own thing" despite what the leader asks them to do. Or their team members roll their eyes while the leader's back is turned in a meeting. Salespeople who lack influence often have difficulty consistently meeting quotas.

Many leaders, salespeople and business professionals I observe and interact with are able to persuade others to take action in the moment, just like the parent in the second scenario. This is influence at its most basic level. These salespeople, for example, are successful making the initial sale but often can't generate repeat sales. Once they stop actively selling, there likely is no ongoing activity.

The dynamics are similar with leaders. You can often tell how much influence leaders have by the way their teams perform when they are out of the office. Are team members just as hard working and productive when the boss is gone as when s/he is in? Another indication of a leader's level of influence is team culture, including how well team members respect and communicate with one another.

The kind of influence I am talking about is impactful beyond the moment. Parents who positively influence their children Monday to Monday® can reasonably expect that their children will usually make good decisions as teenagers and adults, even in their parents' absence. Leaders who embrace this new definition of influence have the ability to change minds, shape behavior and move people to action long after any individual interaction or conversation. These are the leaders whose virtual teams regularly complete projects on time and within budget. These are the salespeople whose customers proactively call when they have a need.

How about you? Are you able to move others to action beyond the immediate moment or interaction?

In the new world of business, your influence has to be bigger than you are. You must be able to influence others to follow your lead and act on your recommendations even when you're not present. This is especially true in an environment where team members and colleagues work virtually or in different locations, and customers are spread across the country if not the world. Your vision and your message must stick with them long after you're gone. When I speak with prospective clients, I know that my influence has to extend well beyond that interaction to a meeting they will have weeks later to choose a speaker, coach or training company. If I am only able to influence them in the moment, my impact will be diminished as soon as we get off the phone.

The goal of every conversation you have, every email, text or social media post you send, should be influence beyond that moment. What can you say or do to have an impact on that individual *three* days, *three* weeks, *three* months, *three* years from now? This is what I refer to as Influence[3], and we will talk about having impact beyond the interaction in greater detail in a later chapter.

Your influence has to be bigger than you are.

Is it really possible to influence someone years after an interaction? Absolutely.

I recently received a call from an individual who attended one of my sessions more than eleven years ago. At the time, he was early in his career and working his way up through the corporate ranks. When I asked why he was contacting me now, he explained that he had been following my blog and social media posts ever since that training session. Now, he has reached a point in his career where his ability to influence others will play a significant role in whether he gets promoted to a senior leadership position. More than a decade after our initial interaction, he is ready for one-on-one mentoring.

How can you achieve that kind of lasting influence? By creating a standout experience for your listeners and readers.

STAND OUT FROM THE CROWD

Not long ago, I was in church with a friend and her five-year-old son, Zachary. As we sat listening to the pastor give his sermon, Zachary started to squirm. After a few more minutes of wriggling, he loudly said, with no filter or volume control, "Mommy, is it almost over?"

My friend shot him that "mother look." It quickly brought back memories of when my sisters and I would get the church giggles and my father would give us that look that told us, "Stop or else . . ." Unlike my sisters and me, Zachary wasn't deterred. He continued to ask when the sermon would be over until finally my friend leaned over and loudly whispered in his ear, "I don't want to hear another word out of you until it's over!"

Zachary scooched down the pew and sat quiet and still, studying his hands. Finally, when he couldn't take it any longer, he sat straight up, looked at his mother and loudly said with all the genuine inquisitiveness of a child, "Mommy, how old will I be when it's over?"

There was a brief moment when you could have heard a pin drop, followed by a wave of chuckles and snickers. Zachary's proud expression communicated how pleased he was with himself that he had made everyone laugh. My poor friend turned beet-red and sank in her seat. Ever the professional, the pastor maintained his composure and continued with his sermon.

Can you relate to Zachary? Have you ever felt the way he did, listening to someone talk–perhaps in a staff meeting, presentation or conference call–wondering with exhaustion, *"When will this be over?!"* Haven't we all felt at some point like a listener held captive?

Is it possible anyone has ever felt that way listening to you?

If you are honest with yourself, the answer is likely a sheepish "yes." As much as you may not want to admit it, you know it's probably true. Do team members check their technical gadgets while you share the latest sales figures? Do you sense that the person on the other end of the phone is distracted or doing something else *while you're talking*? Do you ever notice your friend's or spouse's eyes and mind wandering as you share your excitement from your day over dinner?

Our customers, team members, colleagues and even our bosses are a lot like Zachary in church. Rather than actively listening to us, they are often focused on something else or thinking about when the interaction will be over so they can move on to the next task on their to-do list. You can't hope to impact and influence people if they are counting the minutes until you're finished speaking. It doesn't matter how persuasive your pitch, how valuable your products and services or how critical your message if they aren't listening.

Leaders often have the misperception that if they are giving a presentation or leading a meeting or conference call, people have to listen. You may have the authority to make your team attend a meeting, but you can't make them pay attention. **Physical presence does not equal mental presence.**

In today's business world, you have to earn the right for people to listen to you. You do that by creating a standout experience rather than merely communicating with them. A key element of redefining influence is separating your message from the deluge of information confronting your listeners and readers so that it can be heard, remembered and acted upon.

I'll never forget the medical industry executive who came up after I delivered a keynote speech and told me, "One of our clients recently told us that they would rather get all the details of our services from a lengthy PowerPoint deck than listen to us." Now that is honest feedback that will make you take notice. This is not the kind of standout experience we're looking for!

In any communication, people are influenced by what you say and how you make them feel. You want to connect and engage with them. You want to be certain that what you say is consistent with how you say it. You want to ensure that you're meeting their needs. Too often our communication addresses *our* needs rather than *their* needs.

Influence is not about you. Influence is about the experience you create for someone else based on what they see, hear and understand. That is a key distinction, because it means that responsibility shifts from the listener or reader to the communicator—that is, to you and me.

You have to earn the right for people to listen to you.

Influence is all about *them*, but the responsibility is *ours*.

We bear the responsibility for communicating with influence so that our listeners and readers will be engaged in our interaction. For example, you probably have already picked up on my belief that typos and errors in messages sent from your mobile device diminish your influence. You may even be thinking, "Everyone has typos in emails and texts messages they answer from their phone." Precisely my point! If you choose to live by everyone else's standards, you'll get the same results everyone else gets. Are you okay with being part of the crowd?

Rather than following the standards everyone else abides by, create an experience that sets you apart. Your listeners should never have to work to listen to you. Your readers should never have to work to decipher your emails, text messages or social media posts. How much influence do you have if they can't interpret your meaning? It's your job to write a clear, concise and error-free message. (Want a real challenge? Try creating a standout experience in a 140-character tweet!)

Creating a standout experience for your listeners and readers is the antidote for many influence ills. It allows you to overcome digital distractions, silence internal noise, and capture and keep their attention. It makes you and your message memorable beyond the point of interaction. Creating a standout experience is how you become exceptional rather than merely good and more compelling than the competition.

IT'S NOT ABOUT HOW YOU FEEL, BUT THE RESULTS YOU ACHIEVE

Despite the myth ("I feel influential, therefore I am"), influence is not determined by what you believe or feel about yourself. It's not about how comfortable you feel during a conversation or how confident you are that you wrote a powerful post. Influence is determined by one thing and one thing only: the results you consistently achieve.

True influence produces results.

When you create a standout experience Monday to Monday® and are able to influence others to take action beyond your interaction with them, you will see significant, positive results.

- **If you are a CEO, stakeholders will buy into and support your vision.** A CEO that I coach reached out to me for help when his company went public. He wanted to build a positive reputation and gain influence with his new board of directors so they would act on his recommendations. Through discipline and hard work, he has improved his ability to communicate his vision with confidence and credibility. As a result, he has built a strong, trusting relationship with his board. *Can you clearly articulate and communicate your vision?*

- **If you are in sales, you will cultivate long-term customer relationships, close more deals and put more money in your pocket.** The truth is, we are all in sales, whether we are selling a product, a service, an idea or ourselves. Influence is the foundation for profitable relationships with both external and internal customers. Influence keeps the phones ringing, even in tough economic times. Influence is what drives customers to proactively contact you when they have a need. No matter what you sell, influence is the key to a better bottom line. *Are you closing as many "sales" as you'd like to?*

- **If you are an engineer or in research and development, you will be better able to convince others of the merits of your new ideas and products.** Although engineers and developers are extremely knowledgeable in their areas of expertise, many struggle to sell their ideas to the decision makers, marketing team and sales force. I often coach these professionals on how to enhance their influence and present their ideas so that others understand the value, benefits and features of a product. Having influence can be the difference between a successful product launch and a great product sitting on the shelf collecting dust. *Have you ever had a great idea that you knew was on target, and yet you couldn't convince others of its merits?*

- **If you are a creative type, your pitches to clients will be more powerful and persuasive.** The CEO of an advertising agency recently contacted me. "I cringe when I watch our people pitch to clients," he said. "The message is all about what *they* want to accomplish. They don't ask questions to understand the clients' needs, and they're poor presenters." Another ad exec shared, "Our people believe their work sells itself, and they don't know how to communicate their ideas to meet client expectations." Developing influence gives creatives the skills they need to effectively interact with clients, build trust, ask the right questions and address their real needs. *Does your work really sell itself or could it use some reinforcement?*

- **If you are a team leader, you will be able to clearly articulate goals and objectives, and team members will follow your lead.** Success is based on the results we achieve, and leaders achieve results *through* other people, or, more specifically, through delegation. Delegation is all about influencing people to act on what you want them to do. When you develop the skills of influence, your team will be more productive and engaged. *Is your team following your lead . . . and do they know where you're going?*

- **If you aspire to higher levels of leadership, you will enhance your executive presence and your ability to persuade others to accept your point of view**. When I met Lisa Zarick, she was already successful as the Senior Vice President Director, Learning & Organizational Development at the advertising agency, Leo Burnett Worldwide. She credits her enhanced influence skills with opening doors and helping her land her new position as Executive Vice President of Global Talent Management at Edelman, the world's largest public relations firm. "Developing my influence skills has allowed me to use my expertise, intellectual abilities and confidence in a way that's welcoming rather than like a sledgehammer." As a result, others turn to her and seek her advice more often as the expert and trusted advisor. Growing your influence is crucial to getting where you want to go. *Do you possess the influence and executive presence necessary to lead at the highest levels?*

- **If you run a nonprofit organization or volunteer in your community, you will garner more support for your cause.** Influence is the reason why every nonprofit, movement or community organization would like to have a prominent, powerful or celebrity spokesperson. Success in the nonprofit world is all about getting people to support a cause by contributing their time, talent or treasure. The greater one's influence, the greater one's ability to move people to action. *How would growing your influence benefit a cause you are passionate about?*

- **When you face challenging situations, you will be able to move others to consistently give the discretionary effort that makes an impact.** Executives frequently tell us that with greater influence they are better equipped to lead their organizations through challenging times. One client in particular, a regional director for a national retail chain, took over a new region that ranked near the bottom of the organization. As a result of our work together, she was able to increase her influence as a leader and more clearly communicate goals and strategies to her team. These were key factors in her region climbing from eighteenth to fourth in performance rankings. *How will you handle your next challenge?*

How might increasing your influence get you greater results in your business and career?

It is fascinating to me that our approach to influence hasn't changed much in the last fifty years. Yet updating and upgrading our technology has become a part of life. How do you know when it's time to upgrade your device? When it doesn't serve your needs or work optimally anymore. Influence is no different. If you're not seeing the results you want in your career—or not seeing them consistently—it's time for an influence upgrade.

INFLUENCE IS A SKILL THAT CAN BE DEVELOPED

Several months ago I attended an event at Kellogg School of Management at Northwestern University in Chicago. Before the event began,

everyone in the audience was abuzz, talking about the evening's presenter. Her influence and reputation entered the room before she even
got there.

When the presenter was introduced, she walked onto the stage like
she owned it. As she spoke, she looked directly at each individual in
the audience as if s/he was the only person there. Her style was genuine, funny and likeable. When she spoke about the actions Kellogg was
taking that would benefit the audience members (primarily Kellogg
alumni), her facial expressions communicated passion and sincerity.

After the program, everyone I spoke with commented on her powerful presence and how they admired her commitment to and work for
the School. I knew I had to meet this woman who radiated influence,
and I wasn't the only one! I waited in line for twenty minutes to talk
with her for just a moment. After introducing myself, I shared with her
what I'd heard as well as my own perceptions about her influence. Her
response: "I work on my communication and influence a lot."

This woman keenly understands what I tell clients and audiences all
the time: **Influence is a skill set that can be developed by anyone who
is willing to do the work.** You can grow your influence no matter your
background, position or success to date. The purpose of this book is to
teach you the skills you need to be consistent Monday to Monday®, to
have impact beyond the moment and to create a standout experience.
I am going to redefine influence with very specific how-tos—the same
how-tos I've taught to thousands of leaders across the country. I can
say with the utmost confidence that if you will consistently practice the
skills I give you, you will achieve exceptional results.

At this point, you may be thinking that I missed something. Influence Redefined is Monday to Monday®, beyond the interaction, a standout experience, *built on communication*, based on results and a skill that
can be developed. Where is the communication piece?

Read on to find out why communication is so crucial it gets its own
chapter.

SUMMARY

- Influence Monday to Monday® means that no matter whom you communicate with, what medium you communicate through or when you interact with someone, you are always seen as confident, credible and trustworthy.

- Your influence has to be bigger than you are. You must be able to influence others even when you're not present.

- People are influenced by what you say and how you make them feel.

- Influence is determined by the results you consistently achieve.

- Influence takes work.

CHAPTER 3

LET GO OF WHAT YOU BELIEVE TO BE TRUE

Success requires a deeper understanding of influence.

Which one skill is most important to your success?

Communication.

Are you surprised that the answer is communication?

Perhaps you thought the answer was leadership, adaptability, strategic thinking, problem solving or teamwork. Consider the following:

- **Communication and presentation skills are one of the top C-level skills and traits companies value most,** according to a study conducted by author and Harvard Business School professor Boris Groysberg.[9]
- **Communication was cited as one of the top competencies necessary for success in all leadership** positions (from supervisory through top leadership) in a survey of 332,860 individuals by the Zenger/Folkman leadership development consultancy.[10]
- More than three thousand managers surveyed by the Apollo Research Institute **rated communication as the most important twenty-first century skill.**[11]

You may be thinking: "Some of those points indicate that communication is *one* of the most important skills, not *the* most important."

Fair enough. Let me ask you this: What is the one skill that underlies virtually all other success skills? Think about it: Leadership, strategy execution, collaboration, problem solving, managing change—they all involve communication to one degree or another. You may possess all the necessary success skills in spades, but if you can't communicate with influence, none of it matters. Whether you are expanding your customer base, sharing goals and objectives with your team, creating a financial analysis, implementing a strategic plan, coaching an employee or managing a project, you must be able to speak well, present well and write well. Being strong in one or two of these areas doesn't give you a pass in the others.

Here is more information that might surprise you: A survey of 1,200 companies by Workforce Solutions Group found that while communication ranked as the skill in greatest demand by employers, it was also the greatest shortcoming in applicants. More than 60 percent of organizations surveyed said applicants lack communication and interpersonal skills, a jump of about 10 percentage points in just two years.[12] Another study by Millennial Branding and Experience Inc. found the same result: communication skills are the most sought after by employers, but they are also the hardest to find.[13]

These results reflect what I and my team at Stacey Hanke, Inc. experience in our work. Not long ago I received a call from a prospective client asking me to mentor a high-potential leader they were grooming to be their next Chief Financial Officer. "He is one of the smartest people on our team and definitely has the financial skills to do the job, but his communication skills are holding him back," my contact shared.

When I asked for more details, my contact explained, "His communication is rough around the edges, and with respect to financial information, often confusing. As a CFO, he must have clear and concise communication when discussing the numbers with his peers and board members who may not understand finances the way he does. We want to do everything we can to help him, because he will not be our next CFO if he can't learn to communicate effectively."

I also coached an up-and-coming leader at a large manufacturing company. This individual had years of industry experience and an excellent reputation within the organization. He was known for being reliable and "getting the job done." He had been passed over for multiple promotions because he lacked the ability to communicate with influence.

You may possess all the necessary success skills in spades, but if you can't communicate with influence, none of it matters.

These clients are hardly isolated cases. Many professionals take the quality of their communication for granted because it has been good enough in the past for them to get by. That level of skill won't get them where they want to go in the future.

There is also a flip side to this communication skill issue: Being in a high-level position or achieving a certain level of success doesn't guarantee that you are an effective communicator. The president of a major company once told me, "We don't need to spend money on communication skills because we're already effective communicators." What he didn't know was that his company had confidentially contacted us for coaching, and they felt it was the president who needed the most help.

Cultivating your communication skills gives you a huge double bang for the buck. Not only does developing your communication skills increase the chances you will land your dream job or that next big promotion, it also greatly enhances your influence.

If you want to reach the next level, whatever that may be–progressing from vice president to president, moving from CEO of a smaller company to a larger company, or raising more capital for your entrepreneurial venture–the best action you can take to further your success is to improve your communication skills. (We haven't even touched on the many benefits to your personal life of better communication skills!) The higher you advance in your career, the more influence you need to effectively do your job. Even if all you want to do is stay at the top of your game, you must continually improve. If you're standing still and not moving forward, you're falling behind.

COMMUNICATION: A LOST ART

"We are missing new business opportunities because our people are not effective presenters." "Our poor negotiation skills are costing us money." "Our client relationships are suffering because of our lack of engagement and connection."

These are the types of sentiments I frequently hear from clients and prospective clients. I understand their challenges. In the new world of business, we are quickly losing the skills necessary for communicating in the most influential manner: face-to-face. If you don't use it, you lose it! A senior leader at a Fortune 500 international consulting firm shared with me that she used to frequently facilitate training sessions. Then the scope of her job changed. She currently works remotely out of her home, and communicates virtually with coworkers. "Now when I go to company conferences and events, I often struggle with face-to-face conversations," she confided. "I feel like I'm out of my element because I don't communicate like that on a daily basis anymore."

While technology has given us the ability to communicate more efficiently, we are not communicating more effectively. I wonder how much technology has led to a decrease in the quality of our communication. Not a week goes by that someone doesn't make headlines for a poorly worded or poorly timed comment. Browse through the major news websites, your go-to blogs, your favorite book or magazine, or your inbox, and you'll likely find a number of factual errors, grammatical mistakes, even missing words. Yes, there is a time and a place for BTW, THX, LOL and emoticons, but they are not a part of influential communication.

In today's fast-paced and tech-savvy business environment, communicating with influence has become a lost art. **Great communication**

skills never go out of style. They are just as relevant today as they were twenty years ago, if not more.

COMMUNICATION IS THE "HOW-TO" OF INFLUENCE

Many people think influence comes from power, authority, experience and position. While those factors may affect your influence, they are not the most relevant. That is why I am asking you to let go of what you think you know about influence and embrace what may seem like a radical idea:

Influence is all about your communication.

Communication is the very foundation of influence, but the subject of communication is often missing from discussions about influence. If it is addressed at all, it is usually skimmed over with a simple reference to the need for "clear communication." We take for granted how difficult it is to actually communicate clearly and concisely and how vitally important that skill is. The essential role that communication plays in influence is one of the key distinctions of our new definition of influence, and it is why this discussion about influence is likely different than others you've heard.

The impact of communication on influence becomes even more significant when one considers that we cannot *not* communicate. Virtually everything we do professionally and personally communicates a message and therefore impacts (positively or negatively) our ability to influence others.

In *Contemporary Business*, authors Boone and Kurtz estimate that leaders "spend about 80 percent of their time–6 hours and 24 minutes of every eight-hour day–in direct communication with others, whether on the telephone, in meetings, via email, or in individual conversations."[14] This corroborates the point that communication underlies most other business skills and tasks. Furthermore, this statistic only includes *direct* communication. When we add *indirect* communication (such as writing reports or blogs, preparing for meetings or presentations, etc.), the percentage jumps significantly.

Virtually everything we do communicates a message and impacts positively or negatively our ability to influence others.

In a recent conversation, I asked Jon Finch, Vice President of Training and Recruiting at Milwaukee Tool, about the impact on leaders who do not communicate with influence. His answer was powerful: "Increased time, effort and cost to move the organization. You will have unnecessary meetings about the same issue if you cannot communicate with influence. The unproductive conversations and rework are dangerous to an organization's health and future potential. All of the energy available to move the company forward and work on new ideas will be used up by revisiting previous decisions. Your positive attitude will be drained by managing conflict and negative situations that are not aligned with the organization's vision and strategic goals. Instead of moving forward, you will be wasting time trying to keep the ship afloat."

To fully understand the impact of your communication, consider all the ways you communicate in a day, both verbally and written, professionally and personally. It's astounding when you stop and think about it.

Because we communicate constantly every day, we tend to assume that we communicate well. However, that's faulty logic—the same kind of logic that suggests that someone who drives every day is a good driver or someone who cooks every day is a good cook. We know that isn't true!

Tom Bernardin, Chairman and CEO of advertising giant Leo Burnett Worldwide, sees this phenomenon with others and has experienced it himself. "People think that because they speak in front of groups all the time and aren't nervous about doing it, that means they are good at it. This doesn't mean they are good at speaking, it simply means they're fearless."

We also tend to believe that because we communicate influentially in one situation, we therefore communicate influentially in all situations. In my experience, this is generally not the case, and you likely have painfully observed this as well. Perhaps you have a coworker or leader who delivers effective, influential presentations. When this person facilitates meetings, which are more impromptu and off-the-cuff, you second-guess their communication skills and wonder, "When will this be over?" They may be influential when they need to "turn it on," but not Monday to Monday®.

Most people believe they are better communicators than they are. (Does this sound vaguely familiar?) **If we aren't as influential as we think we are, it's most likely because we're not as effective communicators as we think we are.**

Let's delve deeper into this connection between communication and influence.

THE SIX CHARACTERISTICS OF INFLUENTIAL INDIVIDUALS

What makes someone influential?

Through our presentations and workshops, we ask thousands of people every year that very question. The answers are always the same. Influential individuals are consistently characterized as—

- Trustworthy
- Credible
- Confident
- Knowledgeable
- Authentic
- Passionate

These mini focus groups validate what I have always found to be true, and the executives I talk with also concur. "People want to do business with organizations and people they trust, find credible and have confidence in," said John Gallagher, Executive Vice President of Sales for Loomis Sayles & Company, L.P. "We are in the business of managing money. Why would anyone allow us to manage their money if they didn't trust us and have confidence in us?"

At a basic level, **influence comes from how others experience you**. If others perceive you as trustworthy, credible, confident, knowledgeable, authentic and passionate, they are likely to follow you or act on your recommendations. Conversely, consider the probable outcome if others have a less than positive experience. If prospective customers perceive that you don't have confidence in your product or service, they probably won't buy. If your listeners doubt your trustworthiness because you don't make eye contact with them, they likely won't accept your advice. If your team questions whether you authentically care about their challenges, they probably won't follow your lead.

You have likely heard the popular adage, "Perception is reality." It is absolutely true. Influence is not based on your intentions, but on how people experience you and their perceptions of you.

Consider the power of trust, credibility and authenticity to move people to action. A friend of mine was advised by her dentist that she needed some non-urgent dental work. When she told me she wasn't going to have the work done, she explained her decision: "I had the feeling he was trying to make a buck off of me." Several months later, she heard rave reviews about another dentist and switched to his practice. On the first visit, he recommended the exact same work that her previous dentist had. This time, she agreed. When I asked why she changed her mind, she admitted, "I trust him. I feel like he has my best interests at heart."

I would be willing to bet that both dentists were comparable in their knowledge, skills and abilities and that both dentists truly had good intentions. The difference was that only one had influence with my friend–the one that created a trustworthy, credible and authentic experience for her.

Influential individuals embody the characteristics of trustworthiness, credibility, confidence, knowledge, authenticity and passion. These characteristics describe how you want to be perceived by others if you want to grow your influence. How can you manage other people's perceptions and experiences? Of course, you can never completely control what others think of you, but you have a lot more control than you might think.

How others experience you is determined by the way you communicate. When I refer to communication, I'm talking about the whole package–your words, your presence, your messaging and your nonverbal cues. The words you speak and write convey your knowledge. Your posture and voice reveal your level of confidence. Your willingness to make eye connection impacts your trustworthiness. Error-free communication affects your credibility. Facial expressions and style convey passion. Your word choice, tone and level of interaction communicate your genuine concern and care for your listeners' and readers' needs.

Most business processes–negotiating a contract, closing a sale, customer support or managing employees–are much more complicated than just words. What is the impact on the organization if the communication from the senior leadership team about a new direction for the company is incomplete or inaccurate? What experience does your email create if it takes too long to get

> *Communication refers to the whole package–your words, your presence, your messaging and your nonverbal cues.*

to the point and has a negative connotation? What reputation do you build when your messages are not consistent with your body language?

I often describe the connection between influence and communication this way: **Behind every influential individual sit the six influence characteristics, and behind those characteristics sit effective communication skills.**

Influence is the ability to move people to take action. The way you do that is through your communication. **Your communication either enhances your influence or detracts from it.** This is why the most powerful way to build influence is by improving your communication skills.

INFLUENCE DECONSTRUCTED

My dad is an intelligent man. He has proudly operated a successful farm for fifty-plus years. As a young adult, I became fascinated with the how and why of farming. I was intrigued with how, season after season, he was able to support a family while living under the fickle temperament of Mother Nature. He clearly had a strategy for success, but what was it? How did he know which crops to grow and which kind of cattle to raise? Why did he plant certain crops in certain fields? How did he know the right time to plant and harvest each crop to generate the greatest profit?

As my career in the communications business progressed, that same inquisitiveness resurfaced. I found myself constantly dissecting people's behavior. I was absolutely fascinated by the fact that individuals can execute a certain behavior and not know they are doing it. I watched with curiosity as powerful industry leaders stood in front of huge audiences delivering critical presentations while they unknowingly fidgeted or started almost every sentence with "uh," "um," "so" or "and." I wondered if they realized that many in the audience weren't paying attention to them.

The more I observed, the more I became intrigued with the how and why of communication and influence. How can an obviously knowledgeable individual come across as unknowledgeable and uncertain? How does one's communication impact their results? Why do people think they are more influential than they really are? I wondered, is there a systematic approach for growing one's influence?

I came to the conclusion that I needed a much deeper understanding of what influence is and what lies beneath it. I set out to take influence apart and study its elements. Over the last decade, I've compiled research and extensive learning from our work with clients, as well as my personal best practices, into a **proven method for improving communication and enhancing influence.** The Influence Model, which follows, visually represents this process. It includes the most critical elements for developing influence and the drivers that will sustain influence long term.

The remainder of the book focuses on the elements and drivers of influence with a chapter devoted to each. As a way of introduction, here is a brief explanation of each element:

- **Self-awareness.** How we perceive ourselves is usually quite different than how others perceive us. When it comes to our communication, we don't know what we don't know. We are often unaware of what our listeners and readers actually hear, see and interpret. Self-awareness is the first step to influence because without it, we can't make improvements.

- **Consistency.** To be influential at the highest level, we must be consistent in two key areas. First, our message and our delivery must be in sync. Second, our communication must be consistent Monday to Monday®, meaning that we communicate with influence every day, in every interaction.

- **Reputation.** We can't have influence without a consistently honorable reputation. Reputation represents not only how we define ourselves, but also what others can expect from us. Our reputation precedes us, affecting our influence (either positively or negatively) before we utter or write a single word.

- **Adaptability.** A key element of influence is being able to adapt our message and communication style on the fly to meet our listeners' and readers' expectations, needs and objectives.
- **Impact.** When we connect with our listeners and readers on an emotional level, we give our message momentum. Momentum allows us to make an impact even when we are not physically present.

Each element, starting with self-awareness, builds on the ones before it. Leave one out, and it will be difficult to develop influence. When we embrace all the elements of influence, we are no longer merely good communicators. We become influential leaders, able to inspire people to action long after the interaction is over.

DRIVING SUSTAINED INFLUENCE

Feedback, practice and accountability are what I call the Drivers of Influence. They represent the cycle of continuous improvement that will take you from good communicator to influential leader.

Feedback, practice and accountability are the basis for any kind of skill development. The best athletes are intently focused on how to take their game to the next level and consistently hold themselves accountable to do the work required to get there. They constantly endeavor to improve their performance through feedback (i.e., coaching) and relentless practice. They never stand still. While they may have natural talents and abilities, it is their commitment to continuous improvement that elevates them to the top of their sport.

It is fascinating to me that we readily accept the paradigm of feedback, practice and accountability in sports, yet not in business. The idea that we must continually seek feedback and practice our skills somehow seems foreign in the context of the work world. Just like top athletes, **no matter how good one may be at his or her job, or how influential one may be, there is always room for improvement.**

I once saw magician and comedian Mac King perform at Harrah's Las Vegas during a business conference. After the show, I had the opportunity to observe an interview with Mac that tapped into his expertise. When asked to share the secret of his success, Mac said, "I never take for granted the need to improve. I focus on constant development, never settling for average. No matter how much experience I may have, I can always be better."

Mac began performing at age seventeen and is still honing his skills at fifty-five. Like Mac, the best leaders are always "in school," constantly looking to further develop themselves. "I've never felt like I've nailed it. I certainly can always improve my communication and influence skills," says Todd Spiczenski, Chief Products and Services Officer at Credit Union National Association.

Communicating with influence is a life-long learning process that requires consistent effort and practice. Notice that in the model, the arrows go around the triangle, indicating continuous action. Feedback, practice, and accountability never stop.

Notice too that the arrows point in both directions, indicating that the Drivers of Influence are interrelated. Feedback allows you to

identify which communication skills you need to develop based on your strengths and limitations. Influence comes from practicing those communication skills until they become habits. Accountability is the key to sticking with it long enough to see results. Moving in the opposite direction around the triangle, positive feedback kicks your accountability up a notch. Because you see positive results, you are motivated to practice even more and seek additional feedback.

Feedback, practice and accountability are the process by which we execute the Elements of Influence. In Part II, we will cover each of these three drivers in detail. In Part III, we will explore each Element and how it affects your level of influence. At the end of each chapter, I will provide practical, specific and immediately actionable how-tos designed to improve your communication skills and grow your influence. You will have the opportunity to—

- **Seek feedback**–learn how to ask for meaningful feedback regarding that communication skill
- **Practice**–pinpoint specific ways to practice that skill in your existing daily interactions
- **Hold yourself accountable**–take action to build that skill

Several years ago, a partner at a top-tier professional services firm attended one of our workshops. Afterward, he shared his experience: "I came thinking I was a powerful communicator because I communicate all the time and have received numerous awards. I really didn't believe you could teach me anything I didn't already know. Boy was I wrong. I now realize I'm not as good as I thought, and I have a lot of work to do. Communicating with influence has so many more levels than simply sharing your knowledge."

How about you? Are you thinking I can't teach you anything you don't already know? Are you questioning the true importance of your communication skills?

I challenge you to read on and discover not only the truth about influence, but also just how effective a communicator you really are.

SUMMARY

- Being able to communicate effectively is the one skill most critical to your success.

- Communicating often does not necessarily mean communicating effectively.

- If you want to be influential, others must experience you as trustworthy, credible, confident, knowledgeable, authentic and passionate.

- How others experience you is determined by the how you communicate—your words, your presence, your messaging and your nonverbal cues.

- The Influence Model represents the most critical elements for developing influence and the drivers that will sustain influence long term.

- Let go of what you believe to be true about influence. Remember, you have to let go to grow.

YOU MAY NOT BE AS INFLUENTIAL AS YOU THINK YOU ARE IF . . .
Others don't respond to your emails and texts as frequently or quickly as you would like.

People's response to your emails and texts is based on past experience with your messages. Perhaps your emails are long and confusing, or your text messages are one continuous paragraph rather than brief sentences. Maybe your messages are so abbreviated they might as well be written in Morse code. Perhaps you include people who don't need to be involved in the discussion. Rather than giving your emails and texts the attention you want them to have, your readers' response may be, "Ugh, I don't have time right now to deal with this." Poorly written email and text messages jeopardize your influence. If your messages aren't read, you can't have influence.

Your natural response to this situation may be to—

- Assume your messages are being read even when you don't receive a response
- USE ALL CAPS in the subject line of your emails to try to grab readers' attention
- Send another email or text to make sure your reader received the first one

For Influence Monday to Monday®—

- **Be heard through the clutter.** Before you press send, consider how many emails and texts your reader has received before yours. What can you do to make your message standout from the rest?
- **Be clear, concise and to the point.** Respect your readers' time. Challenge yourself to only use bullet points to communicate key ideas, recommendations and action steps. Ask a trusted peer to review your message and provide feedback on what you need to edit.
- **Hang up the email or text and pick up the phone.** Make an effort to call individuals rather than sending an email or text. Even if you have to leave a voicemail, you lessen the risk of miscommunication. You can follow up with an email or text for documentation.

Part II

THE DRIVERS OF INFLUENCE

CHAPTER 4

INFLUENCE IS A CHOICE

Are you influential by design or by accident?

Years ago, before I started my own company, I worked as a consultant at an international communication training company. As part of this organization's year-long certification process, my presentations were videotaped. By that point in my career, I'd been training and presenting for several years and thought I was a fairly good communicator. After watching several of those video playbacks, I quickly realized that I wasn't as good as I thought.

I immediately hired a speech coach. The first thing he asked after watching and listening to me was, "Would you ever want to sit through one of your presentations?"

Ouch, that hurt! It was tough to admit the truth, but that was a huge step forward in my development as an influential communicator. I've learned a lot since that first punch in the stomach. (And it certainly wasn't my last!)

Have you ever worked with a mentor, coach or personal trainer? It's often a love-hate relationship, isn't it? You hate that they drive you so hard, but you love the results. I have worked with coaches in many different areas of my life–business coaches, speech coaches, vocal coaches, personal trainers and athletic coaches. These individuals constantly pushed me to (and sometimes past) my limits, but the results were well worth the discomfort.

The fastest and most effective way to develop any skill is to seek the guidance of a coach. In their groundbreaking *Harvard Business Review* article "The Making of an Expert," researchers K. Anders Ericsson, Michael Prietula and Edward Cokely state: "You need a well-informed coach not only to guide you through deliberate practice but also to help you learn how to coach yourself.... Having expert coaches makes a difference in a variety of ways. To start with, they can help you accelerate your learning process.... The development of expertise requires coaches who are capable of giving constructive, even painful, feedback. Real experts are extremely motivated students who seek out such feedback."[15]

Business leaders and professionals rely on their influence and communication skills to achieve their goals yet rarely seek advice from those trained to help them improve. If you will allow me, I'd like to be your influence and communication coach. I will show you the steps to hone your communication skills and grow your influence muscle. I will push you to do the work necessary to reap the benefits of having greater influence. Some of the things I will ask you to do may be difficult, possibly even painful for your ego, as I "pull back the curtain" and show you what is really going on with your communication.

A CEO whom I mentored once said to me, "I love you and I hate you." No holding back there! I took it as a compliment that he felt comfortable enough to tell me exactly how he felt. When I asked him why he hated me, he said, "You're the only one in my professional life that tells me how it is."

That is the hallmark of a good coach. They tell you the truth–the good, the bad and the ugly. I will do the same, and I promise any pain will be worth the gain.

If you were going to work with a personal trainer, you would want that individual to be fit and healthy, right? You wouldn't hire a personal trainer that you just saw stuffing themselves at a fast food restaurant. Likewise, your influence coach should be knowledgeable, credible and experienced in communicating with influence.

I've been fortunate to coach senior executives and leaders from around the world. More importantly, I have done the hard work and personally experienced everything you're going to experience through this process. I embrace the idea that a leader never stops learning, and I intentionally work on my communication and influence skills every day.

As your coach, I'm going to ask you to make a commitment to be all-in. Growing your influence requires holding yourself accountable to proactively seek meaningful feedback about your communication and to regularly practice the skills of influence. You can't be *half-in*—accepting only positive feedback or practicing only when it's convenient or easy.

Most people are looking for a quick fix, but there is no quick fix for developing greater influence. You must constantly be taking the steps of the Influence Model. **Becoming a more influential communicator takes serious commitment and discipline.** An executive vice president of a Fortune 500 company that I interviewed agreed: "It takes time and effort to become an influential communicator. You need to work on it every day, and you never really peak."

In "The Making of an Expert," Ericsson, Prietula and Cokely tell us, "The journey to truly superior performance is neither for the faint of heart nor for the impatient. The development of genuine expertise requires struggle, sacrifice, and honest, often painful self-assessment. There are no shortcuts."

COMMITMENT DRIVES RESULTS

Communicating with influence is very similar to living a healthy life-style. Both are lifelong commitments based on daily choices. A healthy lifestyle involves making good choices about diet and exercise: Indulge in a bag of M&M's (I like my chocolate) or eat a piece of fruit? Sit and watch TV or get out and exercise?

Enhancing your influence also comes down to intentional, daily choices: Answer emails during that conference call or use it as an opportunity to practice your influence skills? Assume no news is good news or ask for specific feedback about your communication? Give a canned sales presentation or listen to your prospect and adapt your message accordingly?

When making a decision to pursue a healthier lifestyle, the biggest effort is required up front. Those first two weeks of a new eating or exercise program can be difficult. Once you get over that initial hurdle, though, each choice to work out becomes easier as you create new, positive habits. You soon discover that eating well and working out feel good, and you may even find yourself craving that feeling. The best part? If you are committed, you will typically shed some pounds and inches in the first few weeks.

Enhancing your influence comes down to intentional, daily choices.

The same is true of communicating with influence. It can be challenging at first. You have to be committed to stick with it long enough to replace your unproductive communication habits with effective ones.

Although there are no quick fixes when it comes to communicating with influence, if you hold yourself accountable to seek feedback and practice the skills, you will see positive changes. You will begin to notice how good it feels to authentically connect with your listeners, to powerfully facilitate a meeting and to deliver a message with confidence. The leaders that my team and I coach consistently report seeing immediate improvements. These include noticeable changes in how their team responds to them, increased sales and getting more appointments with prospects and customers.

As you see initial results, your commitment will grow. As your commitment grows, you will be even more willing to ask for feedback and to practice, and you will see even greater results. It is an upward spiral that leads to sustained influence. In time, communicating with influence will naturally become part of who you are and what you do every day, in much the same way that consistent diet and exercise lead to sustained health. When you see the positive results, you will never want to go back to your old habits.

A few years ago, I conducted a two-day "Communicating with Influence" workshop for a specific team within a Fortune 500 insurance company. The participants included directors and above, as well as the leader of this particular team. Six months later, the same group attended our next-level "Boot Camp" workshop.

From the moment the team members walked into the room, I knew they had held themselves accountable to apply what they had learned at the first workshop. Their communication was vastly more influential than it had been when I'd met them six months earlier. When I commented on their transformation to the group's leader, she said, "We made a commitment when we walked out of your session that we were going to be disciplined to do the work, to practice and to give each other feedback."

The results of her team's commitment were obvious. They entered the room like they owned it, with pride and poise. Their messages were clear and concise. Their body language was open, allowing them to instantly connect and engage their listeners. Their presence screamed confidence, knowledge and credibility. The consistency between their message and their delivery established trustworthiness.

One of the workshop participants, the company's chief litigation officer, later told me how the team's commitment had paid off for her personally. "Learning to communicate with influence has built my confidence, whether I'm giving a presentation or involved in an ad hoc conversation. I've also become very observant of what type of communication is effective and what is distracting. When I talk, I notice how my tone affects my message and my listeners." She paused for a moment and then said, "Perhaps the biggest impact is that I've learned that influence is the differentiator between success and failure as a leader."

Make the commitment today to take your communication and your influence to the next level. Like this team and this particular individual, you'll be glad you did.

THE ART OF RESISTANCE

Our clients often ask, "How long will it take to improve my communication skills and increase my influence?"

My response is, "How willing are you to change and how committed are you to doing the work?"

Changing your communication habit is *not* the most challenging aspect of growing your influence. **The most challenging part is changing your mindset.** When you focus on resisting change itself, you can't focus on what is most important: changing.

Not long ago I received a phone call from Olivia*, a client in the financial services industry. Olivia called to ask about one-to-one mentoring. There was nothing unusual about that except that the mentoring was not for her but for one of *her* clients, Barbara†.

Barbara was facing a lawsuit, and both Olivia and Barbara's attorney feared her communication during the court hearings might jeopardize her chances of winning the lawsuit. Thinking they were doing Barbara a favor, Olivia and the attorney offered to invest in a mentor to help Barbara polish her presence and enhance her communication skills. I was happy to help, and we scheduled an initial call for later that week.

When I answered the call at the scheduled time, I was surprised to

....

* Not her real name.
† Not her real name.

discover that Olivia was the only person on the call. "Barbara won't be joining us," she said with disappointment in her voice. "She decided that she communicates just fine and doesn't need any help."

I then suggested we call Barbara so I could share with her the benefits of coaching for even the most effective communicators. "She won't answer," Olivia sighed. "She went to get a manicure instead of joining this call."

That was definitely a first for me! I have worked with many clients who were resistant to improving their communication and influence skills, but none who were in denial to that extent.

What is most surprising to me, however, is not the number of people who are in denial, but the large number of people who understand that they need to make improvements, yet do nothing. We often see this resistance to change with the leaders and executives we work with. (Some are so good at resisting change they have elevated it to an art form.) Resistance to change is understandable. With change comes the unknown. Without change there can be little professional or personal growth.

Throughout my career, I have dedicated myself to studying people's behaviors and habits. How people respond to change lies somewhere on two different continuums that indicate how confident or insecure they are, and how open or closed they are to accepting change. The intersection of these two continuums creates quadrants. Where individuals fall in these four quadrants generally indicates their willingness to change and consequently the level of influence they will be able to develop.

The Resistance Matrix

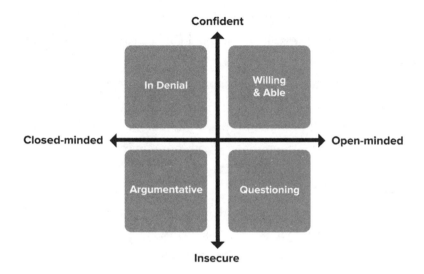

- **In Denial** (closed-minded and confident)–Individuals who fall into this quadrant are quite confident that they are capable of enhancing their skills, but they simply don't think they need to (such as Barbara in the earlier story). Their ego prevents them from seeing that they aren't as influential as they think they are. Unless they are willing to see the truth, they likely will not change.
- **Argumentative** (closed-minded and insecure)–These individuals strongly resist change and tend to disagree with any suggestions for enhancing their communication skills. They believe that anyone who gives them negative or constructive feedback is confused, misinformed or simply doesn't know what they are talking about. Consequently, argumentative individuals will continue to get the same results they've always gotten. Nothing productive happens for those stuck in this quadrant.
- **Questioning** (open-minded and insecure)–Individuals in this quadrant are open to change yet often doubt their ability to make that change. I often picture these individuals as if they

are taking a peek underneath the covers to see if something better is hiding there. This is a step in the right direction because, although uncertain, they are at least willing to learn, grow and change.

- **Willing & Able** (open-minded and confident)–Individuals in the fourth quadrant have the greatest chance of enhancing their communication skills and their influence. Being open-minded and confident is a strong combination for success. Having an open mind is essential if we are to redefine influence. The challenge for these individuals: Are they committed to doing the *work* to achieve influence?

Which quadrant do you fall into? How resistant or open to change are you?

If you fall into the Willing & Able quadrant, congratulations! Your positive mindset is a significant asset. If you fall into one of the other three quadrants, give some thought to how that mindset might be holding you back. Then, read on to find out how you can motivate yourself to change.

THE PAIN AND THE GAIN

Too often in life we stay in resistance until some kind of pain forces us to change, be it physical pain, emotional anguish or regret over lost opportunities. As long as we can live with the pain, we won't do the work required to change. When the pain finally becomes great enough, we stop making excuses and take action. How many people do you know who finally decided to start exercising and eating healthier in response to a health crisis?

The truth is usually obvious in hindsight: if only we had committed to change, we could have avoided all that pain in the first place. Thought leader Jim Rohn once said, "Everyone must choose one of two pains: The pain of discipline or the pain of regret."

Many people don't proactively enhance their influence because they don't clearly understand the pain–or impact–of *not* being influential. As a result, they have no reason to work hard. They don't know that their lack of influence is limiting their career, costing them sales or hindering their results. Tom Bell, President and CEO of Kansas Hospital Association, shared this: "If you're not communicating with influence, people aren't listening to you, you don't have credibility in their eyes and they don't have confidence in you. The cost is huge, both personally and professionally."

Don't get caught suffering the pain of regret in the future because you chose not to do the work now of communicating with influence. Don't allow those moments to occur when your lack of influence catches up with you–when you lose a sale, don't get the next promotion or your team misses a critical deadline.

Calculating the potential cost to your career of not communicating with influence is a powerful way to overcome the inertia of resistance. Another is to focus on the positive benefits of change. When you focus on the gain, you eliminate the internal distractions that prevent you from improving.

Have you ever thought about the benefits to your career and life of having greater influence? How much more could you achieve? Rather than resisting change, imagine how your situation will improve when you begin to communicate with more influence. Focus on—

- Your ideas and recommendations being implemented
- Stronger relationships
- Speaking to be heard and understood
- Increased productivity
- More money in your pocket

The pain and the gain of communicating with influence is like a push-pull force. Understanding the potential pain pushes you into initial action. Recognizing the potential gain generates momentum and pulls you forward into continuous action.

CHOOSE CHANGE

Now that you understand our new definition of influence and you've seen the steps you'll have to take to develop your own influence, you have a choice to make. Will you keep doing what you've always done and continue to achieve the same results? Or are you willing to step it up and commit to doing the work required to improve your communication skills and grow your influence?

I clearly remember a workshop participant who once approached me during a break. "I attended your session a year ago," she explained. "I remember how you emphasized the importance of committing to feedback and practice. You said that if we did not create and put into action a development plan within forty-eight hours, we would never do it, and we would be at the same place a year later."

Then she confessed, "As I sit here today, I keep telling myself if only I had applied what you recommended a year ago, I would be in a much better place now."

One year from today, you will either be at the same level you are now, or you will be an individual who has greater influence Monday to Monday®. Focus on one small change today in how you communicate, and it will move you to the next level of influence.

It comes down to this: How important is it for you to be your very best?

Only you can make the choice to be more influential.

SUMMARY

- The sooner you commit to being all-in to improve your communication skills and enhance your influence, the sooner you will see results.
- Communicating with influence is a lifelong process based on daily choices.
- One of the biggest obstacles to growing your influence is resistance to change.
- Influence is a choice. You have to take action in order to achieve greater influence.

Take Action to Drive Your Influence to the Next Level

Stay motivated to grow your influence by following these three steps:

1. Think about the costs or pain of not communicating with influence in terms of your future professional and personal success. Write your top three on a Post-it® note or index card with the title "Pain."

2. Think about the professional and personal benefits or gain of learning to communicate with influence. Write your top three on a Post-it note or index card with the title "Gain."

3. Post these two Post-it notes or cards someplace where you will see them daily. When you feel your resistance to change rising, review both your pains and your gains to reverse your resistance and keep your momentum moving forward.

YOU MAY NOT BE AS INFLUENTIAL AS YOU THINK YOU ARE IF . . .
People don't follow your lead.

If you are not able to influence people, no one is going to follow you. If they're not following, you're not leading. Do people follow your lead? The proof is in the other person's actions. People may not be following your lead if they don't act on your recommendations or suggestions, do the minimum amount of work to get by, make decisions on their own without your input or limit the information they share with you.

Your natural response to this situation might be to—

- Blame others for not understanding your recommendations rather than accepting responsibility for not clearly communicating
- Become angry with others for not doing what you want them to do
- Focus only on your message rather than the consistency of your message or your delivery
- Communicate aggressively rather than being direct and to the point

For Influence Monday to Monday®—

1. **Check in for understanding.** Many of us make the assumption that if we communicate a message, that message is heard and understood the way we intended it. A message that sounds clear and concise to you doesn't guarantee your listeners have the same level of clarity. If you don't confirm understanding, you run the risk of losing those you lead.

2. **Walk your talk.** Actions speak louder than words. Make sure that what you say is consistent with how you behave and what you deliver.

3. **Seek out feedback.** Ask others to continuously give you constructive feedback. Feedback will keep you on your toes to ensure you are influencing in a way that invites followers.

4. **Be trustworthy.** People only follow those they trust. When your message isn't consistent with your delivery, others will question your credibility and their trust in you will falter. Be conscious of how your delivery habits impact your message.

FEEDBACK

PRACTICE

INFLUENCE

IMPACT

ADAPTABILITY

REPUTATION

CONSISTENCY

SELF-AWARENESS

ACCOUNTABILITY

CHAPTER 5

FEEDBACK:

Fake, Fluff or True?

*Feedback is the gift you don't want to receive but
deep down know how much you need.*

In one of our corporate workshops, I met an executive who used to play professional football in the National Football League. Allan* is one of those individuals you wish you could clone because he is one of the most "coachable" individuals I have ever worked with. Many leaders are open to coaching and feedback, but Allan is over-the-top, bring-it-on, show-no-mercy, ready for coaching.

Allan's attitude toward coaching makes perfect sense. After successfully surviving college football, the NFL draft, year-round training and post-game evaluation of every performance, he has a greater understanding of the importance of feedback than most leaders. He recognizes that feedback and coaching are the foundation of continuous improvement.

Many individuals equate the term "feedback" with criticism and perceive it as negative. I view feedback as quite the opposite. Feedback presents opportunities to better yourself–opportunities you may not

....

* Not his real name.

even be aware of. Feedback polishes any rough edges you might have and brings forth your brilliance. As leadership expert Ken Blanchard once said, "Feedback is the breakfast of champions."

AN UNWELCOME GIFT

With respect to influence, **feedback is someone else's description of your communication, the impact of that communication on them and the consequences of that communication.** The right kind of feedback is the key to learning exactly how you communicate and interact with others. It also reveals how you may be limiting yourself, your influence and your success.

As you will discover in the Self-Awareness chapter, the way you *think* you communicate is different than how others experience you. You may have learned this the hard way, as I have. For example, you may think your emails are thorough; others think you ramble and take too long to get to the point. You may feel confident when you speak, but others experience you as tentative. If you never receive the feedback that your emails are too drawn-out or that you come across as nervous, how would you know you need to make a change?

I often tell the leaders I coach that feedback is the gift you don't want to receive yet deep down know how much you need.

Most people recognize that feedback is essential to development, yet we tend not to welcome it. Perhaps it's because we are afraid of what we may hear. Receiving feedback tends to make us feel vulnerable. We are afraid that our faults—and we all have them—will be exposed. The irony is that most people who spend time with us already know our faults. We are the ones who are often oblivious to them. That is why they are often called our "blind spots."

The familiar saying, "What you don't know can't hurt you," is patently false with respect to influence. The truth is, what you don't know *can* hurt you. Specifically, what you don't know about how you communicate can minimize your influence and negatively impact your career and, ultimately, your success.

Fear can be a great motivator *if* we use it to propel us forward rather than allow it to hold us back. The prospect of *not* knowing our blind spots should be far more frightening than hearing an uncomfortable truth.

Wouldn't you rather know, than not know, what specifically you can do to improve? Constructive feedback is the catalyst for growth. It identifies your strengths and brings to light areas that need improvement. Welcome feedback as the gift that it is.

> *What you don't know about how you communicate can minimize your influence and negatively impact your career and, ultimately, your success.*

DON'T FALL FOR FAKE FEEDBACK

I had the opportunity to interview Neen James, productivity and attention expert and author of *Folding Time: How to Achieve Twice As Much in Half the Time*. When I asked why most people believe they are better communicators than they really are, Neen said, "Because no one gets feedback that they're not."

Even if you routinely ask for feedback, I'm willing to bet that you're not receiving *honest* feedback. The individuals you ask to provide you with feedback are likely sugarcoating their responses—otherwise known as fake feedback—telling you what they think you want to hear rather than the truth.

In an article titled "The Success Delusion," leadership guru and executive coach Marshall Goldsmith points out, "We all want to hear what we want to hear. We want to believe those great things that the world is telling us about ourselves. Our belief in ourselves helps us become successful. It can also make it very hard for us to change."[16]

Sugarcoated feedback is a waste of time and gets you nowhere. You might be walking through life thinking, "I'm good because everyone says I'm good," but is it true? A senior executive once told me, "I thought I was an influential communicator because people tell me I do a good job. I realize now those people are probably lying because they don't have the heart to tell me what's really going on." His words echo what I have heard from many executives.

> *Chances are that you're not receiving honest feedback about your communication.*

Honest feedback is tough to come by for two reasons. First, the higher you are in an organization, the less likely people are to give you truthful feedback about any topic, let alone about your communication skills and level of influence. "I bet you're wondering how I ever made it to the level of CEO," a prominent corporate leader confided in me after seeing himself on video for the first time. Then he thoughtfully added, "I'm guessing my executive team and the entire company is wondering how I made it to this position. Why hasn't anyone ever told me how I come across?"

When you reach a certain point on the ladder, no one wants to tell the emperor he or she has no clothes on. Think about your position. If you are a senior leader, who is going to tell you that you "uh" and "um" your way through a conversation? Who is willing to give you the feedback that you fidget with your pen when you talk? Who is going to tell you that texting in all capital letters comes across as if you're shouting? Lower level team members are understandably reluctant to give candid feedback to more senior leaders who control their performance reviews and compensation.

The second reason fake feedback is so pervasive is that giving and receiving *authentic* feedback can be uncomfortable for both parties. As challenging as it can be to hear constructive feedback, it can be equally difficult to give it. Prospects probably wouldn't be eager to explain that you didn't get the sale because they don't perceive you as being completely trustworthy. Patients and nurses most likely aren't lining up to tell a doctor that his or her bedside manner is lacking.

I once explained to a vice president of human resources at a Fortune

500 company that candid, constructive feedback is an essential part of our workshops and executive coaching. There was a long pause on the other end of the phone. With concern and hesitation in her voice she said, "We are not used to giving or receiving that type of feedback, especially our executives. It's not our culture."

Most people have ingrained in their subconscious mind the adage, "If you can't say something nice, don't say anything at all." This is why you are likely to get fake feedback from your peers, colleagues, leaders and customers. It is much easier for others to give vaguely positive feedback, even if it's not completely true. It is much more difficult to thoughtfully give honest, constructive feedback.

Is it possible there are negative aspects of your communication that you are unaware of and people aren't telling you about?

Fake feedback may feel better for all involved, but it isn't going to get you where you want to go.

TRUST IS THE LINCHPIN OF HONEST FEEDBACK

In order to grow your influence, you need honest feedback, and that requires trust. "The missing link with feedback is trust," shared one of our clients, Steve Richman, President of Milwaukee Tool. "Without trust, you don't get real feedback; rather, everyone tells you everything is great."

When it comes to feedback, **trust is a two-way street**. You must trust that the feedback giver genuinely has your best interests at heart. This allows you to be receptive to the information. The feedback giver must also trust that it is safe to be completely open and honest with you. This is especially true if you are in a position of authority over that person. Leadership guru Stephen R. Covey said, "Leaders, beware! . . . Feedback is your life-support system. Without it, you will eventually fail. Do everything you can to create a culture where it is safe to give you feedback."

Create an environment in which people feel comfortable giving you 100 percent honest feedback.

One of the first steps to enhancing your influence is to create an environment in which people feel comfortable giving you 100 percent honest feedback. Here are a few ideas to get you started:

- **Regularly ask others to give you feedback.** Steve Richman wisely points out, "If you only ask for feedback once a year in a review, the other person is not going to feel comfortable having a dialogue with you about that." The mere act of asking for feedback, and then receiving it well, increases your influence. Others will notice your efforts to improve, develop more respect for you and perceive you as a role model.

- **When receiving feedback, be open-minded and monitor your response.** Fight the urge to be defensive or to make excuses for your behavior. (Remember the Resistance Matrix.) Perhaps you're thinking: "Me? Defensive? Never." When feedback doesn't match our view of ourselves, the natural tendency is to take that feedback personally. The feedback is, after all, about us. Be willing to be vulnerable, to go deeper into that feedback, even though it might be uncomfortable. Be open to hearing some things you might not want to hear, because those are the very messages you need to hear if you want to lead at the highest levels.

- **Carefully consider feedback that seems way off base.** Occasionally you will receive feedback that seems completely inaccurate, even if you're being open-minded. Rather than disagreeing, actively listen and thoughtfully consider the feedback you've been given. If you still disagree, simply thank the person and leave it at that. You don't have to apply all feedback you receive. You are in control of what you do with feedback and whether you decide to change your behavior as a result of it.

If others beat around the bush, seem uncomfortable or give vague answers when you ask for feedback, you likely need to work on building trust with your team.

PROACTIVELY SEEK MEANINGFUL FEEDBACK

Think about the last time you received feedback about your communication. It likely sounded something like this: "Nice job" or "You sounded good" or "That was great!"

We all know this is not meaningful feedback.

I call this type of feedback *fluff* because you have been told nothing. While it may be truthful, it's not helpful because it is vague, generic and safe (i.e., designed to make both you and the feedback giver feel good). You have no idea what specifically sounded good or was great. Was this positive feedback the result of your clear and concise message? Or did it mean you engaged your listeners/readers and kept their attention? How do you know which part of your message was most valuable to your audience?

Much of the so-called feedback we get is really just fluff. Fluff feedback won't provide you with the detailed information you need to enhance your influence. I have been studying communication for more than twenty years, and I've met very few individuals who can honestly say they have received meaningful feedback about their communication skills. **Meaningful feedback is immediate, specific and constructive.** It allows you to—

- Understand how others experience you
- Identify strengths and areas for improvement
- Make changes and see timely results

You owe it to yourself to ask for and receive *meaningful* feedback from others that goes beyond "good job" and a pat on the back. You have to own and drive the process. You must be the one to seek feedback because people are unlikely to give it to you without being asked.

Joseph Folkman is a leadership development expert, behavioral statistician and author of seven books. In a recent study of more than 51,000 leaders, Folkman found that **leaders who ask for feedback are substantially more effective than leaders who don't.** He discovered that leaders who ranked in the bottom 10 percent in asking for feed-back were rated at the bottom 15th percentile in overall leadership effectiveness. Conversely, leaders who ranked in the top 10 percent in asking for feedback were rated at the 86th percentile in effectiveness.

"It appears that being open and willing to receive feedback from others is an essential skill for effective leaders," Folkman concludes. "The best leaders appear to ask more people for feedback, and they ask for feedback more often. Rather than being fearful of feedback, they are comfortable receiving information about their behavior . . ."[17]

Proactively asking for feedback and receiving it openly is a strat-egy for excellence. Sid Chapon, Executive Vice President of Leader-ship and Organizational Development with Leo Burnett Worldwide, understands the value of asking for feedback. "I actively seek feedback from my team and others," he shared. "To make sure that I receive effective feedback and that I can apply what I hear, I ask two simple questions: (1) What worked? and (2) What could I improve?"

Note that Sid asks for balanced feedback. He focuses on both the positives and the negatives of his communication. Understanding and leveraging our strengths is just as important as minimizing our weak-nesses. The feedback Sid has received has helped him to better prepare for presentations. In the past, he approached presentations with an "I can wing it" attitude because he knew the topic and felt comfortable. Now, he talks with his team prior to presentations to learn what points they feel are important so that he can be sure to engage his audience and meet their needs.

The reality is that few people know how to proactively ask for feed-back, receive it well or understand how to apply it effectively. Asking for meaningful feedback is fairly straightforward, but it does take discipline and commitment. You also have to accept responsibility for educating the feedback provider on the specific behaviors you want to improve.

On the next page are six steps to asking for and receiving meaning-ful feedback. Embrace and follow these steps, and you'll be surprised how quickly feedback will propel your development forward.

GIFT WELL RECEIVED

As I've learned firsthand throughout my career, seeking meaningful feedback is often easier than receiving it. How we receive feedback and what we do with it are equally important to our growth.

If you get feedback that is disappointing or doesn't match your self-perception, don't dismiss it. Use it to fuel improvement. (We will talk about practice in the next chapter.) **Influential communicators fail fast.** They don't agonize over their mistakes. Instead, they quickly pick themselves up, make whatever changes they need to make, move forward and avoid stepping on the same landmines in the future. Constructive feedback is a stepping-stone to greater influence.

Six Steps to Meaningful Feedback

1. **Look for everyday opportunities.** Feedback is easier to seek and apply in low-risk, daily interactions rather than high-stakes situations. Instead of waiting for the "big gig," seek feedback on a regular basis. Soliciting feedback involves just a few minutes before and after a conversation, meeting, presentation or even an email.

2. **Go ahead, ask.** Prior to an interaction (e.g., meeting, presentation, face-to-face or virtual conversation), ask someone you trust to observe you and give you feedback. This may be a coworker, mentor, friend or family member. Ask this person to watch for specific ineffective verbal and nonverbal behaviors you would like to change. For example, "I'm trying to avoid beginning my sentences with the word 'so.' Please let me know what you hear." Or, "I'm working on making my emails clear and concise. Please let me know if my writing is unclear or confusing."

3. **Make it simple.** Focus on one behavior at a time. Why just one? First, it is difficult for others to accurately observe multiple areas of communication. Second, if you ask for feedback on multiple items,

Continued

you risk diluting the feedback, becoming overwhelmed and not taking action on any of it.

4. **Dig deeper.** Following the interaction, avoid asking the generic
question, "How did I do?" Instead, ask the person to describe precisely what you said or did. For example, "What behavior did I display that conveyed confidence (or whichever area you are seeking
feedback about)?" If the person responds with generalities such as,
"You did well," ask follow-up questions: "What specifically did I do
that was good?" "What specifically could I do to sound and look
more confident?" "What could I have said to make you take immediate action on my email?"

5. **Clarify.** Summarize to ensure you correctly heard the feedback you
received.

6. **Assess the experience.** After receiving the feedback, consider:
   - How did the feedback differ from your perception of how you
communicated?
   - What will you change as a result of the feedback?
   - How did you feel receiving this feedback?

When the feedback you receive shifts from fake or fluff to meaningful, you will know that your efforts are starting to pay off. Comments
such as "Nice job" or "You did well" will begin to fade. Instead, you
will hear feedback that sounds like "You have the ability to connect
with and engage your listeners" or "You're confident and knowledgeable
about your topic."

When you receive positive feedback, celebrate that success. It is
an indication that you are hitting the "sweet spot" and your influence is expanding.

Gathering feedback is the first step to driving your influence. The
next step is taking action on the feedback you receive.

SUMMARY

- Feedback is someone else's description of your communication, the impact that communication has on them and the consequences of that communication.

- With an absence of constructive criticism and an abundance of false positive feedback, often the notion that we are effective communicators becomes ingrained in our subconscious.

- In order to grow your influence, you must get honest, meaningful feedback, and that requires trust.

- Follow six steps to seek meaningful feedback on your communication.

- Constructive feedback is a stepping stone to greater influence. When you receive positive feedback, celebrate your successes.

Take Action to Drive Your Influence to the Next Level

This week, commit to proactively seeking meaningful feedback on your communication and influence skills in both your professional and personal life. Here are some ideas to get you started:

- Prior to a meeting, explain to the group specifically what you want them to watch for. For example, "I tend to talk to my visual aids, and I frequently look away from my listener's eyes while I'm talking. Would you please give me feedback following the meeting on how often I disconnected with you?" Yes, this puts you in a vulnerable position, but you will quickly enhance your development when you're open to feedback from a group.

- Ask your spouse or a friend to tell you every time you do a distracting behavior, such as fidgeting or excessive gesturing. (For those of you who are in a relationship, I'm guessing these individuals would be more than happy to offer you feedback.) I know what you're probably thinking: The interruptions will quickly become annoying. This is exactly what you want to happen. This kind of instant feedback accelerates your development because it quickly builds awareness. As you become aware of how often you do this distracting behavior, you will begin to stop yourself before you do it.

FEEDBACK

PRACTICE

INFLUENCE

IMPACT

ADAPTABILITY

REPUTATION

CONSISTENCY

SELF-AWARENESS

ACCOUNTABILITY

CHAPTER 6

PRACTICE:

Don't Wait for the "Big Gig"

When it comes to influence, every day is game day.

Apple founder and former CEO Steve Jobs was an incredibly influential communicator. He moved his employees to sustained innovative action, shifted entire industries and compelled millions of people worldwide to buy Apple products.

Jobs was a masterful presenter, and he made it look easy. Perhaps this is why many people think he came by his charismatic style and powerful presentation skills naturally. Carmine Gallo, communication expert and author of *The Presentation Secrets of Steve Jobs*, thinks otherwise. "People who excel in any field work much harder than anyone else. Steve Jobs was no exception. He sharpened his speaking skills over many, many hours of practice spanning three decades. Jobs wasn't born as a great communicator. He worked at it. . . . Hours and hours of practice made Jobs *look* polished, casual, and effortless."[18]

Extensive research backs up the premise that practice is the key to high performance. K. Anders Ericsson is widely recognized as one of the world's leading researchers on the topic of expertise. He and colleagues Michael Prietula and Edward Cokely compiled *The Cambridge Handbook of Expertise and Expert Performance*. This nine hundred-page book contains research from more than one hundred leading scientists who have studied expertise and top performance in a wide variety of areas, from surgery, acting and chess to computer programming, ballet and firefighting.

In *Harvard Business Review,* Ericsson, Prietula and Cokely state: "Consistently and overwhelmingly, the evidence showed that *experts are always made, not born.*"[19] The three researchers conclude that a scientific approach to developing expertise exists and that one of the key elements of that approach is practice (another is working with an expert coach).

Most people believe that influential individuals inherently possess outstanding communication skills and a powerful presence. Yet more often than not, these influential communicators are committed to practice and have put in the work to develop the skills necessary to garner influence.

One of our clients is a well-known pharmaceutical company. During a workshop we conducted for their sales team, the participants consistently raved about the vice president of marketing and what a polished and influential communicator she was. They were convinced that she was lucky enough to have been born with these skills.

During our lunch break, I had the honor to meet this vice president. After I shared with her the reputation she had created, she smiled and said, "If only they knew how much time, effort and work I put into continuously enhancing my communication skills. What people see of me in meetings or on stage is the result of a lot of practice."

Very few individuals are naturally born influential communicators. For the rest of us, **influence is achieved through practice.**

GET COMFORTABLE BEING UNCOMFORTABLE

Have you ever played a sport or a musical instrument or participated in a similar activity? Have you ever been coached in that activity? If so, you can probably relate to the feeling of discomfort that comes from practicing a new skill.

For the sake of example, let's take the game of golf. Imagine that you have been playing golf for a number of years, and you decide to hire a coach to help you improve your game. When you meet with the coach for the first time, s/he asks you to swing the club several times to observe your form. If your golf swing is anything like mine, the coach recommends you take up bowling!

Let's presume you are a better golfer than I am. The coach starts analyzing your swing: "I know exactly what is going on. Your hands are too far apart, you're not pulling the club back far enough, and you're not following through." This is constructive, meaningful feedback. Now you know what you need to do to improve.

When you begin to practice these adjustments, your body feels awkward and uncomfortable. The changes throw you off. Perhaps your emotions are activated, and you become frustrated or defensive. You may even start to question your coach's recommendations. Your subconscious tells you, "This is wrong. It doesn't feel right. Go back to the swing that is comfortable."

If you have experienced something like this before, you know that as you practice over time, your discomfort will decrease. With enough practice, the coach's recommendations become your new normal, and your game is significantly improved.

When we coach individuals to try new influence skills, they often feel uncomfortable. They make statements like "When I pause the silence feels like eternity" or "I feel like I'm staring when I maintain eye connection with one person for a complete sentence or thought."

This may happen to you when you begin to enhance your communication and influence skills. As you practice these new skills, you might feel awkward at first. Your subconscious mind will tell you that if the new behaviors don't feel comfortable, they must not be right. It will try to convince you that your current communication habits are effective because they feel good.

At this point, you have a choice to make. You can revert to your comfortable and secure communication habits. (After all, those habits have gotten you this far in your career.) Or you can roll up your sleeves and do the hard work of practicing the new techniques, knowing any initial discomfort will be worth the end results.

Improving your communication and influence skills requires what high-performance researchers Ericsson, Prietula and Cokely call "deliberate practice–practice that focuses on tasks beyond your current level of competence and comfort." They explained this concept in *Harvard Business Review*: "Not all practice makes perfect. You need a particular kind of practice–*deliberate practice*–to develop expertise. When most people practice, they focus on the things they already know how to do. Deliberate practice is different. It entails considerable, specific, and sustained efforts to do something you can't do well–or even at all. Research across domains shows that it is only by working at what you *can't* do that you turn into the expert you want to become."[20]

Feeling uncomfortable is a completely normal reaction any time we start practicing a new skill that is outside our comfort zone or beyond our current competence. Returning to our golf example, how many people do you think go back to their old form because the new swing is too uncomfortable and to change their swing requires too much work? A lot! How many people have I known who stopped practicing influence skills because it felt a bit awkward or uncomfortable? A lot!

Don't let your temporary feelings determine your outcomes.

Mark LeBlanc, author of *Growing Your Business* and my business coach, often says, "When you get comfortable, you become lazy. Comfort is a sign of needed change." In other words, if you're comfortable, you're not growing. Oftentimes the very things that make us feel the most uncomfortable have the greatest impact.

Change usually involves a bit of discomfort. In order to become more influential, you must learn to embrace it. **Comfort does not equal influence.** It never has, and it never will. If communicating with influence was easy, everyone would do it.

This process is not designed to make you feel good, but rather to make you more effective. Resist the temptation to slip back into your old habits. Don't let your temporary feelings determine your outcomes. If you give in to that subconscious voice, you will settle for being less influential–and less successful–than you could be. If you're uncomfortable, rest assured your influence is growing, and you are elevating your game to the next level.

PSSST. YOUR DISCOMFORT IS *NOT* SHOWING

I am blessed to be able to do the work I do. I have the privilege of watching individuals transform, often right before my eyes. One individual in particular comes to mind–a sales professional that came to one of our "Communicating with Influence" workshops. She was extremely approachable and had great eye connection and a strong executive presence. Yet later when she stood to address the group, she shared, "I am so nervous, I feel like I'm going to throw up. I can't speak in front of groups of more than five people. I get so nervous that my voice shakes and my face turns red. Even my hair shakes."

She made her confession that day in front of thirty people without her voice shaking, her face turning red or her hair moving. (By the way, I've never seen an individual's hair shake, at least not due to nervous energy.) When she watched her video playback, she turned to me with a huge smile and said, "Everything I was feeling was throwing me off. But none of it is real. I can do this!"

During the course of the workshop, she made a huge turnaround from being incredibly nervous speaking to frequently volunteering to present in front of her peers. Imagine if she had never seen herself on video and received that crucial feedback. To this day, she would think that her face turns red and her voice and hair shake when she speaks in front of a group.

What this woman was feeling was dramatically different than what her listeners were experiencing. This is known as disparity–the incongruity between how you feel and how you appear to others.

Try this quick experiment (you've likely done this exercise before, although perhaps not in this context): Cross your legs and look at which leg is on top. Now, uncross your legs and cross them again with the other leg on top. Do you feel a bit awkward or uncomfortable? Most people do. I guarantee that no one sitting in the room with you would know that you are uncomfortable.

Developing communication and influence skills allows your authentic self to come through.

When you begin to practice new communication and influence skills, your subconscious mind will tell you that if you feel uncomfortable, your listeners will also perceive you as being uncomfortable. This is rarely true. This is a critical concept to grasp. **When you understand that your discomfort is not seen by your listeners, you will be more likely to stretch beyond your comfort zone.** Two of the biggest obstacles to enhancing your influence are your feelings and your mind. If you allow them to run the show, you will stay stagnant.

Clients often express to me their concern that they will come across as stiff, clumsy or inauthentic while practicing new communication skills. What many of these individuals don't realize is that they already come across that way to their listeners. A common mistake is to equate being uncomfortable with being inauthentic. In truth, there is no correlation.

This process is not about turning you into someone different. It is not going to turn you into a robot or change your personality. Instead it allows your authentic self to come through. Your unconscious communication habits may actually be distracting your listeners and readers and preventing them from seeing and hearing the real you. Enhancing your communication and influence skills helps you to develop and express your unique communication style.

When you start practicing these skills, your listeners and readers will absolutely notice a difference—a positive difference. They may not always be able to put their finger on what has changed, but they will sense something . . . a real connection, a masterful communicator, an influential leader.

EVERY DAY IS GAME DAY

Good news! Your boss just asked you to share your team's best practices at the company's upcoming leadership conference, which is one month away. You make a note on your calendar to start preparing for your presentation two weeks before the conference. You will need to get your slides together, and of course you will want to practice the presentation a few times too. By the time the big day arrives, you should be ready to give a top-notch presentation, right?

If you wait until you need them to begin practicing the skills of influence, it will be too late.

When I receive calls from clients requesting that I coach their sales team right before a big sales presentation, I decline. I know that if I recommended changes without the team having significant time to practice, it would result in more harm than good. They would probably end up using my name in vain during their sales presentation.

Professional athletes don't start practicing a week or two before the playoffs or championship game. They understand that delivering their best performance in the big game requires months, if not years, of consistent daily practice. Athletes and teams that don't practice regularly never even make it to the big game. The best athletes practice year round, and the elite treat every day as if it were game day.

You can't start practicing communication skills a few weeks before the "big gig" and expect to hit the ball out of the park. As I said earlier, influence is not something you can simply turn on for important events. To reach the big leagues of your profession, you need to practice the skills of influence every day. You play the way you practice.

Don't wait until you need them to start practicing the skills of influence.

Daily practice is crucial for several reasons:

1. **Practice makes permanent.** Top athletes practice to the point where they can perform at peak levels on autopilot on any given day. That is where you want to be–able to communicate with influence Monday to Monday®, at any time, in any situation. You have to start now and hold yourself accountable to practice regularly in order to create the muscle memory that will make those skills automatic.

2. **Low stakes = low risk.** It is more straightforward and less stressful to correct ineffective communication habits in lower-risk situations such as impromptu hallway conversations, routine emails, text messages and dinner-table discussions. It is much more difficult and nerve-wracking–and often more costly–to correct bad habits when the stakes are high. There are no second chances in critical conversations, investor meetings and must-win sales pitches. You can't stop in the middle of a major presentation and say, "I didn't come across the way I wanted to. Let me try that again."

3. **Influential leaders have ever-expanding comfort zones.** Influential communicators are committed to doing the work to enhance their influence, knowing any initial discomfort will disappear with practice. If you don't practice influence skills every day, the level of discomfort never diminishes. It's as if you are starting over every time you decide to practice. With daily practice, your comfort zone grows ever larger, and what was once uncomfortable becomes your new normal.

4. **The more you practice, the faster you become an expert.** Based on their extensive research, Ericsson, Prietula and Cokely introduced what has become known as the "10,000 hour rule"–the idea that it takes 10,000 hours of practice for an individual to truly master a particular skill.[21] If you only practice before "big gigs," you will likely never master the art of communicating with

influence. Even if you practice for recurring meetings and presentations, it would take decades to become proficient. With daily
practice, you will become an exceptional communicator, and your
influence will grow rapidly.

When you practice your communication skills daily, you are also
building your presentation skills. If you only practice for the "big gigs,"
your presentation will likely sound memorized and scripted. Delivering
a big presentation breeds feelings of fear and dread for many people
because we think of presentations as being different from our daily
communication. In reality, we are presenting, selling and influencing
others to take action every day through many mediums: face-to-face,
virtual, meetings, email and text messages.

A leader from a large pharmaceutical company had a big a-ha
moment during one of our mentoring sessions: "I get it! A presentation
is really an extension of a conversation." He hit the nail on the head.
How we show up for every conversation and interaction determines the
level of influence we have, rather than simply turning on our "A game"
for presentations.

Practice drives success. **The greater the desired outcome, the
greater the demand on practice.** Business coach Mark LeBlanc wisely
says, "What you do every day is more important than what you do once
in a while." True influence is Monday to Monday®. For greater impact
and influence, treat *every day* as game day.

NO TIME TO PRACTICE? NO PROBLEM.

I can almost hear you now: "Stacey, I'm already busy. There is no way I
have time to practice every day." I get it. If I had a dollar for every time
I've heard that same sentiment from the leaders I work with, I'd be
sitting on a beach in Tahiti.

The good news is that communicating with influence does *not* require you to carve out more time from your already hectic, over-scheduled days. That is one of the most powerful aspects of this process. I'm not asking you to do something in addition to all the things you're already doing. **I'm asking you to consciously practice communicating with influence in the interactions you're already having.**

If you have spoken to anyone or sent even one email or text today, you had an opportunity to practice. When you look at it this way, practice becomes part of your daily routine. The opportunities are right in front of you, just waiting to be used.

Practicing communication and influence skills is like eating healthier. It's all about making intentional choices. Every time you eat is an opportunity to choose a healthier option. With just a little more conscious effort (and some willpower), you can choose a piece of fruit, for example, instead of candy-coated, dark-chocolate M&M's (my favorite). It doesn't take more time to choose and eat the fruit. You're simply being intentional about something you're already doing.

You communicate all day, every day. Take it up a notch by being intentional about what you say and how you say it so that you will have more influence in that interaction. Be conscious in your communication rather than sprinting through your day, having conversation after conversation, shooting off email after email, never giving a second thought to how your communication impacts your influence.

Cassandra Farr, Region Leader for GE Healthcare, has cultivated her influence through committed practice. "When I leave someone a voicemail, I record that voicemail several times before I send it. I listen to it and ask myself, 'Would I want to listen to this voicemail? Would I respond to it? Would I act on it?'"

Her practice has paid off. C-suite executives regularly return Cassandra's calls. If you have ever tried to get a busy executive to return your phone call, you know what a challenge that can be!

The big secret to growing your influence is to leverage your existing activities as opportunities to practice. Everyone has time to improve their communication skills because every meeting, conversation, phone call, email and text message represents a chance to practice. There are probably hundreds of practice opportunities in any given work day, plus many more in your personal interactions.

The Law of Accumulation was first proposed by eighteenth-century economist Adam Smith as an economic law of capitalism. It refers to the accumulation of profits which are put back into production to create increasing productivity.[22] In recent years, it has taken on a more general connotation: A small thing accumulated over time becomes a big thing.

With respect to influence, I define the Law of Accumulation as this: **Small amounts of daily practice accumulated over time lead to big results.** If you will practice a little bit every day, the compounding effect on your level of influence and consequently your results will be dramatic. If you were to practice a new communication skill just three times a day in the midst of all your professional and personal interactions, just think how much faster you could reach that critical 10,000 hours where true mastery occurs.

Being influential through every word you speak and every movement you make Monday to Monday® takes practice. That's it . . . practice. You can't read how-tos in a book, attend a training session or rely on your title to be influential. The

The big secret to growing your influence is to leverage your existing activities as opportunities to practice.

hard truth is that being influential is a lifelong journey of practicing through day-to-day interactions.

This may not sound easy, and it's not. Stay with me, and I will lead you through critical steps to help you stay committed to daily practice.

SUMMARY

- Influential communicators are not naturally born, but grow from consistent and diligent practice.
- Growing your influence involves embracing the initial discomfort that often comes with practicing new skills.
- Don't wait for the "big gig." Treat every day as game day so you will be able to communicate with influence at any time, in any situation.
- Every interaction is an opportunity to practice.

Take Action to Drive Your Influence to the Next Level

In Part III of this book, I will give you specific skills to practice for each of the Elements of Influence. In the meantime, start flexing your influence muscle now. Identify a few behaviors you will commit to practicing daily. For example—

- To honor your listeners' time and be true to your word, begin and end your meetings, and face-to-face and virtual conversations on time, as promised.
- To make a real connection, only speak when you see your listener's eyes, and pause (stop talking) when you look away.

YOU MAY NOT BE AS INFLUENTIAL AS YOU THINK YOU ARE IF . . .

You typically run out of time before you've made your key points.

In a well-crafted message, your key points are essential to getting your listeners to act on what you have to say. If you run out of time before you unveil these takeaways, your listener's cups are only half full. They don't have the critical information they need to make a decision and take action.

Many communicators run out of time because they don't adequately plan, prepare and practice. As a result, they ramble and take too long to get to the point. Or they get carried away in the moment and focus on what *they* want to discuss rather than what their listeners need to hear.

Your natural response to this situation might be to—

- Speak faster to try to cram in as much information as possible
- Go over the time allowed, disrespecting your listeners' time
- Keep talking and hope you'll eventually communicate your point

For Influence Monday to Monday®—

1. **Identify your listeners' needs ahead of time.** What is the most critical information your listeners need to know in order to take the action you want them to take? Plan to cover that critical information first and fill any remaining time with supporting material.
2. **Practice.** As you prepare for and practice your presentation, plan for 20 percent less time than you will be given. Be sure to practice with a timer. If your presentation runs long, start cutting!
3. **Regroup and refocus.** If you discover you are running out of time, pause briefly to gather your thoughts and decide which information you absolutely must communicate in the time remaining. Then explain to your listeners that the forthcoming information will be vital.
4. **Respect your listeners' time.** One of the biggest mistakes presenters and facilitators make is to go over their allocated presentation or meeting time. This communicates to listeners that their time is not valuable. If you cannot cover all of your key points in the allotted time and the discussion must continue, ask your listeners if they want to dedicate more time now or if they prefer to schedule a future date to continue the discussion.

FEEDBACK

PRACTICE

INFLUENCE

IMPACT

ADAPTABILITY

REPUTATION

CONSISTENCY

SELF-AWARENESS

ACCOUNTABILITY

CHAPTER 7

ACCOUNTABILITY:

Eliminate Excuses and Take Action

*It's not the skills and techniques you learn that make you
more influential. It's what you DO with what you learn.*

One of the most common questions I receive from clients is, "What
can we do to make sure our team members apply the influence skills
and techniques you've taught us?"

When I share suggestions for how they can help hold their teams
accountable for growing their influence, I often hear the same response:
"We've tried holding our teams accountable in the past, and it didn't
work. What else do you suggest?"

I'm tempted to respond, "Hmmm . . . a shock collar?"

All joking aside, accountability is a serious matter. I've come to realize that communicating with influence–like succeeding at anything in
life–really is quite simple. It comes down to accountability and follow-through. To increase your influence, you need to hold yourself
accountable to do the work of seeking feedback and practicing. You
need to commit to digging deeper for specific feedback or to practicing

during that routine phone conversation. This is where the rubber meets the road.

Through my work, I meet many people with all different types of personalities. Almost universally, they struggle with accountability and follow-through. I get it. I'm not perfect when it comes to accountability either. Holding oneself accountable to consistently take action can be difficult.

Why is it so difficult to follow through on our commitments to ourselves and others? Most of the time, we *know* what it is we should be doing. It's the *doing* that trips us up. What happens in this knowing-doing gap that prevents us from following through? In my experience, there are three barriers to accountability:

- We too easily let ourselves off the hook with excuses.
- We lack sufficient self-discipline.
- We think we have to achieve our goals alone.

Influential communicators eliminate excuses, discipline themselves to hone their skills every day and reach out to others for support. One of my CEO clients stated, "We underestimate the level of discipline, focus and accountability that's necessary to improve our communication. We all want an easy answer. There's nothing easy about committing to do the work no matter how tough it gets."

Influential communicators eliminate excuses, discipline themselves to hone their skills every day and reach out to others for support.

Clients routinely tell me that their most significant challenges in taking their communication from good to influential are getting over the initial hurdle and slipping back into their old habits. My goal with this chapter is to help you overcome the difficulties most individuals experience when they begin to focus on communicating with influence. If you can hold yourself accountable to do the initial work, things will start to click and your influence will quickly grow.

WHAT EXCUSES ARE HOLDING YOU BACK?

I don't have time to exercise because I'm too busy. If I didn't travel so much, I could eat healthier. If other people hadn't gotten us off track, I could have ended the meeting on time.

Do any of those statements sound vaguely familiar? I'm sure you have never said anything like that. I know I haven't. (Yeah, right!)

One of the biggest threats to accountability is making excuses. I could write an entire book on the excuses I've heard over the years from people who say they want to be more influential but then don't do the work required to get there. These excuses often take the form of blame, deflection or rationalization: *We missed the deadline because some people on my team don't do what I ask. I didn't get the promotion because the other candidate has a friend in senior management. I didn't make the sale because the prospect doesn't have the budget.*

Sometimes these assessments are accurate; sometimes they aren't. More often than not, team members don't act on what we say because we don't clearly communicate our expectations. Sometimes we don't get the promotion because we lack the influence a higher leadership position requires. Perhaps we lose the sale because our message focuses on our product rather than discovering and solving our customers' problem.

When we don't get the results we want, it's all too easy to rationalize or convince ourselves that our excuses are valid. **Making excuses allows us to ignore the hard-to-hear truth that we just don't have the influence we think we do.**

I also hear lots of excuses for why people don't seek feedback and practice:

- *I've got too much on my plate this week. I'll start asking for feedback on Monday.* Procrastination usually indicates resistance to change. As the saying goes, "When you're looking for an excuse, any one will do."
- *I don't have time to practice.* What? This person never communicates? As we discovered in the last chapter, we all have

numerous interactions throughout the day when we can practice influence skills.

- *I don't often speak in front of people, so this doesn't apply to me.* If you
  communicate with others either verbally or in writing as part of
  your job, this applies to you.
- *I'll try,* which really means, *I won't follow through.* This is a
  pre-excuse in anticipation of possible failure. Eliminating the
  word "try" from your vocabulary automatically increases your
  accountability.

What excuses are holding you back from growing your influence?

As you have read the initial chapters of this book, perhaps that little voice in the back of your mind has been telling you all the reasons
why you can't increase your influence. The first step to accountability is
to identify and banish those excuses. Excuses move you backward rather
than forward. When you accept your own excuses, you limit the opportunity for positive change. I have personally witnessed the differences
between individuals who make excuses and those who commit to action.

The next time you find yourself making an excuse or rationalizing a
less-than-desired outcome, stop! Instead, take responsibility. Hold
yourself accountable by looking at your own communication or behavior rather than blaming someone or something else.

> *Hold yourself accountable by eliminating excuses and looking at your own communication rather than blaming someone or something else.*

For example, instead of
pointing the finger at team
members for not following
your directives, ask how you
could have more effectively
communicated your expectations or better managed the
project. Rather than accepting the notion that your prospect doesn't
have the budget to buy your product, take a hard look at your sales presentation and determine if it truly addressed their needs.

Avoid letting your excuses rule the day and determine your future.

When you eliminate excuses and invest your energy into action, you make changes that guarantee greater results.

SELF-DISCIPLINE IGNITES ACTION

I learned about self-discipline and accountability from my parents. For sixty-six years, they have been dairy farmers in Wisconsin. Being a dairy farmer is an incredibly tough job. Every cow has to be milked every day at sunup and again at sundown. My parents milked 105 cows twice a day, 365 days a year, for decades. There were no days off. The cows had to be milked on holidays, birthdays, sick days, frigid days and sweltering days. My parents disciplined themselves to do the daily work of their profession. Over time, it became ingrained in the very fabric of who they are.

When I talk about accountability, I am asking you to discipline yourself to do the work of communicating with influence every day until it becomes ingrained in you. Fortunately, this commitment doesn't involve physical labor like it did for my parents. It is as simple as consciously thinking about influence any time you're involved in an interaction—simple but not necessarily easy.

It is challenging to stay focused on communicating with influence in the midst of the daily grind. It takes discipline to communicate with influence at the end of a long staff meeting, while answering emails at 4:30 on a Friday afternoon or when responding to an after-hours text from a customer. You might be tempted to let yourself off the hook when you are especially busy or stressed. Instead, honor the commitment you made to yourself to grow your influence. Honor your integrity by doing what you said you were going to do—no matter the circumstances, regardless of how you feel, even when no one is watching.

Leadership expert John C. Maxwell has said, "Discipline is doing what you really don't want to do so that you can do what you really want to do." That is precisely what Pat Hatler, Chief Legal Officer with Nationwide, discovered.

"For several months after attending your workshop, I was convinced

I wouldn't be able to break my old communication habits," Pat shared. "I needed to walk the talk with my team, so I made a personal commitment. It was all a matter of discipline and practice. In time, the changes in my communication became second nature, and I began to see how effective these skills can be."

One way to increase your self-discipline and accountability is to get crystal clear about what you want to achieve. When you have clarity about your influence goals, you will have a better understanding of the effort required to achieve them. The greater the desired outcome, the more discipline that is required. If you will constantly keep your influence goals top of mind, discipline will come a bit easier. **Success is certain when you start with self-discipline.**

FIND AN ACCOUNTABILITY PARTNER

People who write down their goals, share their goals with a friend, and send weekly updates to that friend are on average 33 percent more successful in accomplishing their goals than those who simply articulate their goals.[23]

These were the findings of a fascinating research study by Dr. Gail Matthews, Psychology Professor at Dominican University of California. Dr. Matthews studied the impact of accountability on goal achievement in the workplace. Participants in the study were randomly assigned to one of five groups, with each group building on the actions of the previous groups:

- Group 1 simply thought about their goals.
- Group 2 also wrote down their goals.
- Group 3 also wrote an action plan for each goal.
- Group 4 also shared their goals and action plans with a friend.
- Group 5 did all of the above and sent a weekly progress report to the friend.

At the end of the study, the participants rated their progress toward their goals. Group 1 participants accomplished only 43 percent of their goals. In comparison, those in Group 4, who shared their goals and plans with an accountability partner, accomplished 64 percent of their stated goals. The participants in Group 5 who also had weekly updates with their accountability partners were by far the most successful, achieving 76 percent of their goals.[24]

Working with an accountability partner is a powerful strategy for developing communication and influence skills. An accountability partner is someone to whom you are willing to be accountable for your development. It is similar to working out with a personal trainer or training partner. An accountability partner will give you constructive feedback, encourage you to step outside of your comfort zone and push you to do the work of growing your influence.

When you share your influence goals with others, you are more likely to follow through on your commitments and less likely to make excuses or slip back into your old habits. "If no one is measuring your development, you won't hold yourself accountable," explains Jill Tomalin, Chief Operating Officer of Credit Union National Association. "Anything that is measured and watched improves; anything that isn't measured will deteriorate. For example, I will have a stronger interest in holding myself accountable if I know my boss is closely measuring and watching my development."

You will also achieve better results when you are accountable to someone other than yourself. I am part of two mastermind groups, and I work with a business coach. These individuals are my accountability partners. Every Friday afternoon, we share by email what we accomplished that week. Knowing that I have to write that email on Friday increases my accountability to set goals and work toward them every day.

Another key reason to work with an accountability partner is because you can't do this alone, and I mean that literally. When it comes to our communication and influence skills, most of us are unconsciously incompetent. We don't know what we don't know. The way we think we communicate is typically not how others experience us. If we want to improve, we must work with someone who will give us honest, meaningful feedback about the strengths and weaknesses we aren't even aware of. (To learn more about how to work with an accountability partner for maximum value, download our free resource at www.InfluenceRedefined.com.)

> You will achieve better results when you are accountable to someone other than yourself.

An accountability partner can be anyone you trust who is willing to hold your feet to the fire. It could be a mentor, peer, coworker, friend or family member. Your accountability partner doesn't have to be someone you are friends with, but it does need to be someone you respect. Ideally, you would have one accountability partner in your professional life and one in your personal life, because you want to be influential in both. My business coach holds me accountable professionally, and my sisters do the same for me personally.

Many of our clients have had success with reciprocal arrangements where two leaders serve as each other's accountability partners. Todd Spiczenski, Chief Products and Services Officer with Credit Union National Association, told me about his accountability partnership. "A colleague and I agreed to coach and critique each other when we are doing any type of presentation. Working with a peer really helps me not only to stay focused on the areas I want to improve, but also to stay accountable for improving."

Pat Hatler's team at Nationwide decided to be accountability partners for one another. "We went through your workshop as a team, so we all had the same experience. We therefore don't have any excuses to not keep influence skills and techniques front of mind. During our monthly meetings, I always make a point to have the team talk about what is working for us. When we observe each other present or communicate in a meeting, as a team we give each other specific feedback on how we did. As a result, accountability has come naturally for our team. Everyone appreciates how much more effective they are when they're better communicators."

Some sales organizations require their sales teams to participate in videotaped role play as part of their initial sales training. Why not keep this commitment going? If you are in sales, find another salesperson and agree to be each other's accountability partner. If you really want to see improvement, at least once a month, role-play a sales scenario while your accountability partner videotapes you.

The sooner you find an accountability partner, the sooner you will see results. Although accountability ultimately rests with you, there's nothing wrong with getting a little help from people you can trust. "An accountability partner is like a tornado," shared thought leader Neen James. "It's the energy of combining two great minds to give you momentum and results."

ACCOUNTABILITY CHECK

You are beginning to understand that communicating with influence takes focus, discipline and a lot of hard work. **Now it's time for an accountability check.** Have you held yourself accountable to implement the action items from the last two chapters? Have you asked someone to give you meaningful feedback? Have you practiced a new, simple influence skill? If not . . . why not?

If you are serious about growing your influence, stop right now and complete the action steps in the feedback and practice chapters (if you haven't already), as well as those that follow. Then get ready to pull back the curtain and discover for yourself what is really going on with your communication. Self-awareness is the first element of influence.

SUMMARY

- Accountability is one of the most difficult aspects of influence; yet without it, influence will never happen.
- Hold yourself accountable by accepting responsibility for your level of influence and your communication habits.
- Put your energy into improving your communication rather than making excuses.
- Influential communicators discipline themselves to develop their skills every day until they become habit.
- You will achieve greater results when you are accountable to someone other than yourself.

Take Action to Drive Your Influence to the Next Level

Holding yourself accountable is difficult if you don't have a game plan. A professional athlete wouldn't even think about entering a game, match or race without a strategy for winning. As a professional, you are competing to be heard, to be understood and to have influence. Create your personal **accountability game plan by following the four simple steps that follow.** (Solidify your commitment by writing down your plan in the spaces after the steps now.)

1. **Eliminate excuses.** What excuses are keeping you from growing your influence?
2. **Set goals.** What are your top three goals for communicating with influence this year? How important is it for you to achieve these goals? What are you willing to do to achieve them?
3. **Find an accountability partner.** Who will you ask to be your accountability partner? Choose someone whom you feel comfortable receiving feedback from and who will tell you the truth about what is really going on with your communication. Examples: leader, coworker, friend, or family member.
4. **Decide how often you will meet with your accountability partner.** Examples: once a week after your team meeting for fifteen minutes; every other week for one hour in person or virtually via video conference; monthly for lunch. If you cannot meet on a weekly basis, I recommend a weekly accountability email. Every Friday

afternoon, send an email to your partner sharing which influence skills you have been working on, how you are practicing, the results you are seeing and what you commit to do the following week.

Need more support? Take 5® is a one-year online mentoring program designed to help you stay motivated and focused and hold yourself accountable for developing influence skills. For more information, see the back of this book or www.staceyhankeinc.com/take-5/.

Part III

THE ELEMENTS OF INFLUENCE

CHAPTER 8

SELF-AWARENESS:

How You Unknowingly Sabotage Your Influence

We can only change our behavior if we are first aware of it.

I never cease to be amazed by the things people do while they are communicating. I have seen just about everything:

- The CEO who grasped the side seams of his pants and slowly pulled up his pants legs;
- The senior executive who continuously twirled her scarf;
- The director who moved his head from side to side like a bobblehead toy;
- The vice president who built paper clip sculptures;
- The accountant who talked about how excited he was to be working at his company while his facial expression looked like he was in pain;
- The engineer who, thinking he was keeping his listeners engaged, walked from one side of the room to the other, stopping each time in the middle to move 360 degrees, a circle, before continuing;
- The vice president who waved his pen between his fingers (until the day the pen flew out of his fingers, across the table and hit another executive in the forehead).

What is most fascinating to me about these situations is that these individuals were completely unaware of what they were doing. Granted, the above examples may be extreme. Yet I promise you, these are not isolated incidents. The majority of leaders I work with have distracting communication habits that they are unaware of: quirky behaviors, odd facial expressions (or no facial expressions at all), over-gesturing, body language that is out of sync with their words, conversation littered with filler* words, or writing in all capital letters.

"Leaders often believe they are better communicators than they really are because they focus on what they are saying and not how it is being said," shared Karen Eber, Business Learning Leader, Energy Connections at General Electric. "They aren't aware of all the things that interfere with the message they think they are delivering. When they speak, people are too distracted by how they are speaking to notice what is being said."

Distracting communication habits sabotage our message and minimize our influence. Most of us have at least one communication habit that is distracting to our listeners or readers. Do you ever put your hands in your pockets during stand-up conversations? If so and you have anything in your pockets like keys or coins, I would be willing to bet that you begin to play with them. You likely aren't aware you're doing it, but to those around you, it looks quite interesting to say the least.

> *Distracting communication habits sabotage our message and minimize our influence.*

People communicate the way they do because they simply don't know any different. They are unconsciously incompetent. They are not aware of how they communicate, and they often don't have the tools to address any areas of weakness even if they were aware of them. This entire book boils down to essentially two things: (1) getting you to become aware of how you communicate and (2) giving you the tools to make positive changes in your communication in order to become more influential.

....

* Filler words include *uh, um, so, but, however, actually, well, now, basically, like, you know, okay,* and *right.*

More than likely, your communication is sabotaging your influence without you even knowing it. That is why self-awareness is the first step to greater influence.

TOP 10 DISTRACTING BEHAVIORS . . .	AND WHAT THEY COMMUNICATE
Looking away from your listener while you're talking	Untrustworthy
Fidgeting with fingers, pen, clothes, slide clicker, etc.	Nervous, uncomfortable, uncertain, lack of confidence
Shifting your body side to side or forward and back	Uncomfortable, lack of confidence
Pacing back and forth	Nervous, searching for content
Placing your hands on your hips	Aggressiveness
Using filler words	Nervous, uncomfortable, lack of knowledge
Voice trailing off at the end of sentences	Unsure, uncomfortable, insecure
Speaking too softly	Uncomfortable, lack of confidence, lack of knowledge
Speaking too loud	Brashness, egotistical, offensive
Over-gesturing	Overly anxious

KNOW THYSELF

Many of history's greatest philosophers as well as many contemporary leadership experts have talked about the importance of "knowing thyself." Self-awareness is often seen as a *soft skill* that is definitely a plus but not a necessity for leadership success. **The leader who ignores the wisdom of self-awareness limits his or her potential.**

"There is *one* quality that trumps all, evident in virtually every great entrepreneur, manager, and leader. That quality is **self-awareness**," says Anthony Tjan, founder of venture capital firm Cue Ball and co-author of the *New York Times* bestseller *Heart, Smarts, Guts, and Luck*. "Self-reflection and its reward of self-awareness cannot be thought of

as passive exercises, new era meditation, or soft science. They're absolutely essential."[25]

Recent research also validates the significance of self-awareness.
One quantitative study found a direct relationship between leader
self-awareness, leadership effectiveness and organizational financial
performance in the form of rate of return on corporate stock.[26]

Self-awareness is a critical leadership skill because it brings clarity. Self-awareness leads to acceptance, understanding and, ultimately,
action. Without self-awareness, you can't recognize your communication strengths and weaknesses, or your "super powers" and "kryptonite"
as Anthony Tjan describes them. Without self-awareness, the rest of
the Influence Model doesn't work. Each successive step is based on your
being keenly aware of your actual communication behaviors.

I should warn you that this critical first step of gaining greater
self-awareness requires you to be open-minded, vulnerable and committed. **Influential communicators acknowledge that they don't
know everything, and they are open to self-discovery.**

In researching material for this book, I had the opportunity to talk
with Lou Heckler, professional humorist and speaker, and coach to
other professional speakers. "Most people believe they are better communicators than they really are because they deceive themselves into
thinking they already know it all," he told me.

Then Lou shared an insightful story. He was on a plane sitting next
to a psychologist. After some small talk back and forth, Lou asked him,
"What is the secret to improvement? Who among your clients really
and truly gets better?"

The psychologist smiled and said, "The ones who are willing to
embrace their own ignorance."

How about you? Are you ready to discover what you don't know
about your communication? Are you willing to accept the truth about
what your listeners and readers already know?

LET FACTS, NOT FEELINGS, BE YOUR GUIDE

A few years ago, I mentored a new female executive. Through her company's leadership surveys, it had become apparent that there was a significant discrepancy between how this executive viewed herself and how her team perceived her. She believed she presented herself to others as an open, welcoming person. Yet on the survey question that asked, "Do you consider your leader approachable," only 18 percent of her team gave a positive response. (Her predecessor received an 89 percent positive response on the same question.)

During our first session together, the disconnect became clear to me. When this leader communicated, even one-on-one, she appeared cold and indifferent. She had no facial expressions, her voice was monotone, and her body language indicated she was closed off. She genuinely felt that she was approachable.

Through our coaching sessions, she gained self-awareness and understanding of what her listeners experienced when they communicated with her. With feedback and practice, she became a more influential leader. Her team members began to open up to her and be more receptive to her ideas. As a result, she gained their respect, and their team meetings became more productive.

In my work with thousands of people across the country, I am constantly surprised at how many executives, salespeople and professionals are not aware of how their communication is experienced by others and how much that impacts their ability to consistently produce results. After seeing himself on video, a leader attending one of my sessions shared, "I always considered myself an effective communicator until I saw and heard myself on video. I was shocked by how different I felt compared to how I came across. If people knew how their communication was really perceived, they would be appalled."

It is natural human tendency to base our opinion of ourselves on how we feel when we communicate rather than the facts of how we actually look and sound. Our thinking is, I feel good, therefore I am good. More often than not, what we feel inside doesn't translate to what listeners are seeing and hearing. We may feel that we are better communicators than others think we are. Or the opposite may be true. Others may see us as better communicators than we think we are, like the woman who thought her face turned red and her hair shook when she spoke in front of a group.

To enhance your influence, you need to evaluate your communication based on facts, not feelings. You need to get to the heart of what is really going on by experiencing your communication through the eyes and ears of your listeners and readers.

There are two primary ways to get the facts about your communication and grow your self-awareness. One we have already talked about in-depth—proactively seeking meaningful feedback. Getting feedback from others is an essential part of improving your communication and enhancing your influence. It can be all too easy to discount or rationalize constructive feedback that is significantly different than what you feel is true about yourself.

5-Minute Feedback

One of the best ways I've found to increase my self-awareness and focus my efforts is to use what I call 5-Minute Feedback. 5-Minute Feedback enables you to quickly and effectively identify your communication strengths and weaknesses and then apply what you've learned in your very next interaction. A quick tutorial and complimentary 5-Minute Feedback form can be downloaded from www.InfluenceRedefined.com.

The other way to get factual data about your communication is to watch yourself on video or listen to yourself on audio. Video and audio recordings allow you to observe firsthand your communication behaviors and actions captured live in the moment. They provide an unmatched level of self-awareness because they enable you to step outside of your perceptions about yourself and understand how those differ from reality.

Video in particular is the ultimate form of factual feedback. **Video acts like a mirror, enabling you to see exactly what others see and hear exactly what others hear when you communicate.** What you see and hear is who you truly are when you communicate.

We tend to see ourselves as better communicators than we actually are.

Video allows us to see and hear ourselves as our listeners see and hear us.

I know what you're probably thinking: "Why would I want to put myself in an uncomfortable position by videoing myself?" Few individuals like seeing themselves on video. Video invites vulnerability, which often means discomfort. Without that moment of truth, you are seriously limiting your potential for success.

When was the last time you recorded yourself speaking on video or audio? If it wasn't within the last six months, there is a strong probability that you don't know the facts about your communication. If you have never videotaped yourself, I guarantee that you are unaware of your communication habits. I don't mean to offend you or be disrespectful. I am simply being honest with you. I consistently hear from the executives I coach that I am the first person who has told them the truth about their communication. If you are investing the time and energy to read this book, then I owe it to you to tell you the truth too.

If you do nothing else that I suggest in this book, video record yourself speaking.

Video recording yourself is the only way I know to reveal the truth of what your listeners see and hear. As painful as it might be to watch and hear yourself, is it any worse than spending the rest of your career clueless as to what others are thinking about you or saying about you behind your back? As much as you might not want to do it, videoing yourself is one of the greatest investments you can make in your life, both professionally and personally.

THE MIRROR DOESN'T LIE

Many years ago, a participant approached me after a presentation and said, "You gesture too much. It's really distracting."

I tried to graciously accept his feedback. In my head, however, denial quickly set in. "What a jerk!" I thought. "He knows nothing about presenting."

Some time had passed since I had last video recorded myself, so I thought I had perfected my delivery. (I was young in my career and oblivious to the truth that we never perfect our communication.) I thought I was entertaining, confident and knowledgeable, because that was how I felt when I spoke. I had no idea that my audiences found me entertaining to a fault.

I couldn't stop thinking about what the participant had said. Several months later (yes, it took me that long to overcome my denial), I decided to video myself again. I wanted to prove him wrong.

I felt like an idiot when I watched the playback. The video showed me the cold hard truth: that participant had been right on the money.

Everything that I thought enhanced my delivery in fact distracted my listeners and detracted from my message. I thought my gestures and energy created interest and impact. The truth was that my arms never stopped moving, and my energy was over-the-top. I thought I was good at making eye contact, when in reality my eyes scanned the audience like a lawn sprinkler. I thought my communication was clear and concise, yet I was completely oblivious to the constant flow of filler words that came out of my mouth and how I talked in paragraphs.

Watching my video playback was extremely uncomfortable. It was difficult for me to understand how I could have been so unaware of how I looked, how I sounded and how I must have been perceived by my audiences. I even watched the playback again and muted the sound. I couldn't deny the truth with the proof staring me in the face.

The self-awareness I gained by watching that video playback changed my career. I had been clueless as to how I truly communicated and how I and my communication were experienced by my

Video never lies and never sugarcoats the truth.

audiences. While watching it was certainly difficult, I am glad I did. Finally, I understood what my listeners already knew about me.

When you watch your video playback, you will discover your unique communication traits. Video provides the feedback that tells you what you need to practice. You will be able to easily identify your strengths and areas for improvement. For instance, you may feel confident when you speak, but discover that your body language suggests uncertainty. You may be enthusiastic about the product or service you are promoting, while your facial expressions and energy level inadvertently convey boredom. Perhaps you speak clearly and concisely, but your gestures look stiff and forced. You may be the smartest person on your team about a particular subject, but you lack brevity and lose listeners' attention. You may be genuine and authentic, but you never look your listeners in the eyes to build trust.

Video never lies and never sugarcoats the truth. It also reveals the lies we tell ourselves about our communication. It is fairly easy to dismiss a less-than-positive critique from a peer or colleague. It is much more difficult to reject what is right there in front of you.

THE TURNING POINT

Every individual who attends our workshops and coaching sessions is videotaped in various communication situations, such as presentations, meetings, sales calls and face-to-face or virtual conversations. When individuals view their video playback for the first time, they tend to have a similar experience. Most people–about 70 percent–are surprised at the difference between how they think they communicate and the reality. I often ask participants the same question my speech coach asked me years ago: "Would you want to listen to you?" Ninety percent say "no."

The initial shock of seeing how one truly communicates can be a bitter pill to swallow, particularly for senior leaders. Bob Raidt, Executive Vice President at Leo Burnett, told me, "Seeing yourself on video is jarring. It crushes your subjective perception. However, most things worth doing force you to step outside of your comfort zone. This is how you really achieve more influence."

An engineer for a well-known consumer products company shared, "I always thought the more I talked, the smarter I would look to my listeners. I now realize that's not true. I don't even know what I'm saying in the video. If I don't understand what I'm saying, how can anyone else understand me?"

Sometimes participants are pleasantly surprised by what they see on video. "It wasn't as awful as I expected," said Jill Tomalin, Chief Operating Officer of Credit Union National Association. "I could clearly see what needed to be tweaked, and it all seemed doable. If you're not getting these insights, you can easily be oblivious to your flaws."

For those who want to be more influential, seeing themselves on video is typically a turning point. Once they have time to process what they have seen, most accept that there is room for improvement and are ready to change. Sometimes, when individuals don't like what they see or hear, they move into denial or defensiveness and make excuses for why they look or sound the way they do. Here are some of the more common excuses I hear:

- *If I had time to prepare, I would sound more confident.*
- *I don't fidget when I'm comfortable.*
- *I have more enthusiasm when I'm talking about a topic I'm passionate about.*
- *I have good eye contact when I'm speaking to just one person.*
- *I only talk fast when I'm in front of a group.*

When I hear these kinds of excuses, I recommend we record the participant again under different circumstances. In almost every case, the behaviors the individual showed in the first video are repeated in the second video. Our communication behaviors are generally consistent in all areas of our life, regardless of the circumstances, audience, how well we know the material or how well prepared we are.

When the way we *think* we communicate is emotionally tied to our identity, it can be challenging to separate the two. I will never forget the time a female executive who I was mentoring insisted that her video playback was not her because that was not how she thought she sounded. "That is not me," she said, dead serious. As I looked at the video and then back at her, I said, "Then who is it? This person sure looks like you."

Our communication behaviors are generally consistent, regardless of the circumstances.

If I have not convinced you by now that videoing yourself and observing your playback is absolutely critical to enhancing your influence, the remainder of this book will not provide you with value. Don't waste your time if you're not ready to invest in yourself, because any efforts to enhance your influence will fall flat until you see for yourself what your listeners truly see and hear.

CHANGE YOUR COMMUNICATION BEHAVIORS . . . CHANGE YOUR RESULTS

Have you ever bought a new car and then noticed that you see that same car everywhere on the road? It is not because dealerships suddenly sold hundreds of the same car you purchased. Those cars were always out there; you just never noticed them until you became aware of that make and model by buying it.

The same concept applies to communication and influence. **When you identify your ineffective communication habits through video and/or audio, you will automatically become more cognizant of those habits in your interactions.**

For example, you might discover by watching yourself on video that you initially make eye contact with your listeners and then look away. You observe that this creates the perception that you lack confidence or might not be completely trustworthy. The next time you are in a conversation and look away from your listener, you automatically will be more aware of that behavior. You will likely catch yourself and re-establish eye contact.

Recording yourself ramps up your self-awareness, much like exercising ramps up your metabolism and makes it a more efficient fat-burning machine even when you're not exercising. After recording yourself and watching the playback several times, you will be more acutely aware of your communication and influence in every interaction. **You will become a more effective communicator and more influential, even when you are not actively practicing.**

People are often surprised when they learn that we videotape every workshop participant and coach every individual. They usually ask something like, "Doesn't that require a great deal of time and effort?"

My response: "Yes, it does. We do it because self-awareness is the catalyst for change, and video is the absolute best tool for creating self-awareness. It exposes the communication habits that detract from your message, minimize your influence and sabotage your success. Change those behaviors, and you'll change your results."

Now that you have gained critical self-awareness about your communication habits, you can begin to focus on having consistency Monday to Monday®. Consistency is the next critical element of influence.

——————— SUMMARY ———————

- Distracting communication habits can sabotage your message and minimize your influence, often without you even knowing it.

- Self-awareness is the first step to greater influence.

- How you feel during an interaction is not the same as how your listeners perceive you.

- Let facts, not feelings, be your guide—you must see yourself through the eyes and ears of your listeners.

- Communicating with influence will require you to video yourself and watch the playback.

- If you find yourself making excuses for your communication behaviors, you might be in denial.

Take Action to Drive Your Influence to the Next Level

Make a commitment to increase your self-awareness by recording yourself and watching/listening to the playback. Only you can make it happen. You have to be all-in! Following are some quick tips.

1. **Recording:**
    - There are numerous opportunities to record yourself in action: presentations, team meetings, phone calls, face-to-face or virtual conversations, community and volunteer events.
    - It is quick (takes about ten seconds) and easy to record yourself with either video or audio on your smartphone, tablet or computer if you don't have access to a video camera. If you have kids, I can almost guarantee you've videoed them using your smartphone, so no excuses!
    - If videoing yourself during a presentation or meeting, increase your credibility by explaining to your audience, "I'm recording my presentation today because I am constantly working to develop my communication skills" or, "Part of my commitment to my professional development is to see and hear myself through your eyes and ears."

- If audio recording yourself during a phone call, only record your side of the conversation unless you specifically ask permission to record the person on the other end.

2. **Playback:**
   - Immediately following the event or interaction, watch the video or listen to the audio playback. Immediacy is crucial so that you can more easily compare how you felt to what your listeners saw and heard.
   - Watch and listen from your listeners' viewpoint. Trust what you see and hear. Believe what the video shows. Nothing is more honest.
   - Give yourself feedback by answering the following questions:
     - » *Is there a difference between how you felt during the recording and how you look?*
     - » *What perception would you have of yourself based on what you see and hear?*
     - » *Would you be influenced by your communication?*
     - » *What do you want to change?*
   - Use the Self-Awareness Checklist (free download at www.InfluenceRedefined. com) to help you evaluate your message and body language, such as movement, eye connection, gestures and facial expressions.

3. **Action:**
   - Document the specific actions you will take in order to improve your communication and grow your influence using the Self-Awareness Checklist.
   - Hold yourself accountable to practice the behaviors and skills that need improvement in your daily interactions.

YOU MAY NOT BE AS INFLUENTIAL AS YOU THINK YOU ARE IF . . .
You are frequently interrupted.

Most people believe they get interrupted because that is simply how the interrupting person behaves. In reality, the blame more often lies with the speaker rather than the interrupter. Your listeners may be interrupting you because you take too long to get to the point or because you never pause to let them get a word in edgewise.

Your natural response to this situation might be to—

- Jump in and interrupt the interrupter
- Continue talking over the interrupter
- Allow the interrupter to take control of the conversation

For Influence Monday to Monday®—

1. Get to the point quickly. Oftentimes, the more you say, the more you confuse and frustrate your listeners. As their patience runs out, they interrupt to try to get the information they need from you. Remember, less is more!

2. Focus your passion. When we are passionate about a topic, we often feel compelled to tell our listeners everything we know about it. We think our listeners will be as passionate about it as we are. This is rarely true. Share your passion while keeping your message directed.

3. Pause to listen and give the person time to speak. An influential communicator understands that the power of persuasion involves saying less and listening more.

4. Consider the interruption a gift. An interruption is actually a friendly reminder that you need to get back on track or adapt your message to your listeners' needs.

INFLUENCE

IMPACT

ADAPTABILITY

REPUTATION

CONSISTENCY

SELF-AWARENESS

FEEDBACK

PRACTICE

ACCOUNTABILITY

CHAPTER 9

CONSISTENCY:

Does Your Message Sink or Swim?

Consistency is the difference between a
good communicator and one with true influence.

What if the future of your career hinged on a single interaction?

On the TV show *Shark Tank*, budding entrepreneurs' futures are determined in a matter of minutes by their product pitch to a panel of self-made multimillionaire and billionaire investors called "sharks." Each entrepreneur is hoping to secure an investment from one of the sharks to take their business or product to the next level and potentially become millionaires themselves. If none of the sharks are persuaded to invest, the entrepreneur leaves empty-handed.

If you have ever watched the show, you know that the sharks can be quite tough on the contestants. While much of their critique is about the viability of the products being pitched, they also offer very direct feedback about the entrepreneurs' presentation and delivery:

- *"You're rambling. You don't sound like you understand your plan."*
- *"Your pitch is horrible. You should have stopped before you started."*

- *"Why didn't you give us specifics up front rather than dance in circles?"*
- *"You're not answering the question."*
- *"I don't trust you."*

Comments like these are usually followed by the panelists' famous words, "I'm out!"

Real estate mogul Barbara Corcoran is one of the sharks. How does she size up each entrepreneur? In an interview with *Success* magazine, she shared that one of her strategies is to watch the entrepreneurs' body language during their pitch to see if they have "the right stuff." Do they sweat, fidget, maintain eye contact? Most don't cut it. "I'm out on two-thirds of them right there," Corcoran said.[27]

Consistency is often the difference between success and failure. In this case, it's consistency between an entrepreneur's message and how that message is delivered. Those whose message matches their body language and delivery will be more likely to influence the sharks to bid on their ideas. Those whose nonverbal cues undermine their message are often left out in the cold.

Whether you are facilitating a meeting, delivering a high-stakes presentation, making a sales or creative pitch or having a virtual or face-to-face conversation, you are pitching your ideas. Similar to the *Shark Tank* contestants, how well you present and communicate those ideas to others has a significant impact on your ability to get what you want and need to grow, both professionally and personally.

COMMUNICATING BEYOND THE WORDS

Influence comes down to two different elements that often collide: what you communicate, or the message, and how you communicate it, or the delivery. The message encompasses the verbal part of communication—the words you speak or write. The delivery represents the nonverbal portion—all the ways you express yourself apart from the actual words.

Delivery can be broken down even further into visual and vocal cues. Visual cues are the way you present yourself, including how you dress, your presence, body language, posture, gestures, facial expressions and eye contact. Vocal cues have to do with how you sound, such as tone of voice, volume and pitch.

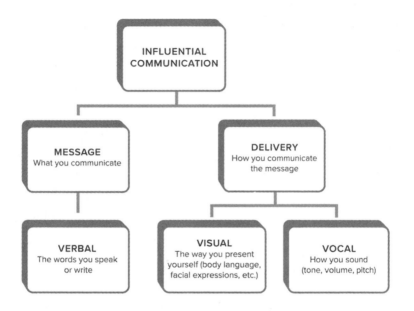

In our work with leaders across the globe, I find that it is rarely their message that is the problem. The majority of individuals we coach are knowledgeable when it comes to sharing their expertise on their products, services, jobs and industries. The challenge is usually that their delivery sabotages their message. Individuals who are bright, honest and have something meaningful to say are often misjudged, misinterpreted or dismissed because of their ineffective nonverbal communication. Even the best of speakers can have their words undone by a grating tone, awkward body language, odd facial expressions or timing that isn't quite right.

"Most people understand the message they want to convey, but it isn't always relayed in the same manner in which it is intended," shared Whitney Bullock, Quality Manager at John Deere Horicon Works. "They may be unaware of the signals their body language is sending."

I still remember one attendee in particular from a workshop years ago. It was the first time he had ever been videotaped while speaking. We asked him to talk about a work project he was currently involved with and then to speak for a few minutes about what he liked to do in his personal time. We do this because we want to observe how individuals communicate when they are talking about an area of their life they're passionate about. Typically their energy will increase, their face will light up, and they will have more volume and inflection in their voice. We then coach them to use those same behaviors when they communicate about other topics.

After talking for a moment about a work topic, this individual began to speak about his family. He told the group about his beautiful wife who had stayed with him through some tough times and his three amazing little girls. He talked about how special their family vacations were to him and the places they loved to go. While sharing these stories, his voice was cold and flat, and his face was devoid of any emotion or expression. Observing his nonverbal cues made us all question how he really felt.

When he watched the video playback, he said, "If my family saw that they would think I was going to leave them." I didn't hesitate to agree with him! His message and his delivery were dramatically out of sync. If he wasn't able to convince his coworkers how much he loved his family, what chance did he have of influencing a room full of salespeople to buy into his new marketing strategy?

Most of us are focused on content only and don't pay enough attention to our delivery. Think about the last time you were in a high-stakes conversation. What were you more focused on—what you were saying or your posture, facial expressions and tone?

"In the past, I would spend hours preparing my message and visual aids. I never spent any time practicing and focusing on my delivery," a senior leader recently confessed after observing himself on a video playback. "I was convinced that my work and knowledge alone would influence my listeners to take action. Now I know I've been missing a critical element to influence—my delivery."

Your listeners only know what you tell them and what you show them. Therefore, be careful what you tell them and show them. Influential communicators ensure that their message and delivery are consistent Monday to Monday®. Their energy level matches the nature of their message. Their gestures are purposeful rather than distracting. They connect with listeners rather than focusing on their notes or slides. Their posture and body language suggest they want to engage with listeners rather than give a monologue.

Being fully aware of what your body language, facial expressions, eye connection, physical mannerisms and vocal tone communicate are essential to influencing those around you. Most individuals aren't even aware that their message and their delivery are out of sync.

> *Influential communicators ensure that their message and delivery are consistent Monday to Monday®.*

This is why self-awareness is the crucial first step to greater influence. It shows us—sometimes in brutal fashion—where our message and delivery don't match. The good news is that when we are aware of inconsistencies, we can change them.

AUTHENTICITY IS INFLUENTIAL

Prospective clients often ask me how Stacey Hanke, Inc.'s coaching and training are different from that of other communication training companies. I explain that communicating with influence is about so much more than crafting a powerful message and honing delivery skills. Messaging and delivery are just two pieces of the puzzle. Communicating with influence is authentically connecting and engaging with listeners and readers Monday to Monday®.

Similarly, when we begin workshops or coaching programs, participants often share their concern that they will have to conform to scripted or canned presentation techniques. We assure them that we are not out to change who they are and that communicating with influence is not about inserting the right gesture at the right time. It is quite the opposite.

Your listeners want you. They just want the best you.

Influence involves finding your authentic communication style and learning to use that style Monday to Monday® in every interaction and through every medium.

Have you ever observed an individual you personally know deliver a presentation and suddenly become someone else? Their presentation mannerisms and delivery are so different from their one-on-one communication style that you question their authenticity.

Too many leaders have been sucked into the illusion that they need to go into "presentation mode" for high-stakes interactions. This is not where influence occurs. Influence results from the cumulative effect of all your interactions. Having different communication personalities for different communication situations actually diminishes rather than enhances your influence.

People value honesty and transparency. They want to know that you sincerely care about them and their concerns and that you will help them get there. Your listeners and readers want you. They don't expect you to be perfect. They just want the best you. When the way you communicate day-to-day is as confident, credible and trustworthy as the presentations you deliver, your listeners will appreciate your authenticity.

Being an influential communicator means being genuine. It means using gestures that come naturally to you in a purposeful rather than distracting way. It involves understanding when to use that great smile or natural humor. It is learning to harness a confident voice in order to be respected and heard. It means communicating with brevity and clarity while still coming across as conversational.

Leaders often secretly reveal to me, "I always thought I needed to be more serious than I really am" or "I'm concerned that my listeners won't take me seriously if I use facial expressions." In the quest to be what you think your listeners want, you jeopardize your influence. Every leader can communicate with influence while hanging on to their authenticity. Case in point: although all of the instructors on my team utilize the skills of influential communication, each individual has his or her unique style.

Being authentic, natural and letting your personality come through actually enhances your influence. When you try to be someone that you're not, you can't deliver that person consistently. Be your best you, Monday to Monday®.

TRUST IS WHERE INFLUENCE OCCURS

You may not have ever thought about consistency being such a critical element to influence. It is crucial, and here is the reason why: People will only allow you to influence them if they trust you.

In an earlier chapter, we talked about how influential individuals are consistently characterized as trustworthy, credible, confident, knowledgeable, authentic and passionate. Trustworthiness is consistently cited as the most important characteristic of influential individuals, and it is closely tied to two others: credibility and authenticity. If others trust you, they will often look past a lack of confidence or passion and even forgive a lack of knowledge. Without trust, influence cannot occur.

People will only allow you to influence them if they trust you.

Stephen Covey, one of the world's foremost leadership authorities, organizational experts and thought leaders, said, "Trust is the glue of life. It's the most essential ingredient in effective communication. It's the foundational principle that holds all relationships."

Trust expert David Horsager believes everything is built on trust, from financial institutions to personal relationships. "Whether you are a student or a CEO, a teacher or a parent, a politician or a nurse, trust multiplies influence and impact."[28]

A popular business maxim says that people do business with people they like. I disagree. Does it help if they like you? Of course. It is quite possible to be liked and not trusted. (Do you have any friends whom you enjoy going to dinner with but would never take advice from?) People do business with people they trust.

People are influenced by what you say and how you make them feel. If your message and delivery are in sync, others will perceive you as trustworthy, credible, sincere and authentic. When your words match the way you behave, how you look and how you sound, your communication is the total package. What your listeners hear, see and feel is in harmony. Consistency builds trust, which in turn builds influence.

In his bestselling book *The Trust Edge*, Horsager refers to eight pillars of trust. Not surprisingly, consistency is one of those pillars. "The little things done consistently make for leaders being followed, increased sales and retention, and a higher level of trust. Consistency is the way brands are built and character is revealed."

Clarity is another of Horsager's trust pillars. "People trust the clear and mistrust or distrust the ambiguous."[29] When your message is not consistent with your delivery, you raise doubt in people's minds. Listeners may feel confused and question your trustworthiness. As Horsager points out, "Skepticism brings everything into question, slows processes, and promotes suspicion."[30]

You have probably experienced this yourself. Have you ever been in a meeting in which someone is recommending some type of action but they sound hesitant or express hesitation through their body language? How likely are you to follow their recommendation?

I once coached a senior leader in the research and development department of a global confections manufacturer. This individual had a PhD and had received numerous awards for both his innovative ideas and the execution of those ideas. The first time I observed him present to a small group of investors, I began to question his expertise. He rocked back and forth, fidgeted with his fingers and began every other sentence with "so." His facial expressions were lifeless as he stated, "Our new strategy is absolutely critical to the growth of our business and client relationships." He looked and sounded like he didn't believe one word of what he was saying, although I'm certain he believed in his strategy wholeheartedly.

You can be the most knowledgeable individual in your industry, but it doesn't matter how smart you are if you're not able to communicate in a way others can understand and trust. People will hear your message if you communicate it well. If you communicate it well and have their trust, they will believe.

If you find that you lack credibility, it could be because your message and your delivery send conflicting signals. Your listeners hear one thing, but see something altogether different. If your listeners perceive that you do not believe in your own recommendations, you will not be taken seriously and you certainly won't be able to influence them. If *you* don't believe you, why should they?

MESSAGE VS. DELIVERY . . . WHICH ONE WINS?

If I, um, tell you that, uh, it is really critical, you know, to be like consistent in all your interactions, would you like really have confidence in my, you know, expertise?

Now, imagine me torturing you with that sentence with my hands shoved in my pockets, no eye connection and a closed posture. Would you trust and believe what I was telling you?

When we send a conflicting message—our message and our delivery are not consistent—what are our listeners inclined to believe? In the battle between message and delivery, which side wins?

Professor Albert Mehrabian is a pioneer in the study of communications. Unfortunately, his research has been heavily overused and frequently misinterpreted as the idea that the majority of spoken communication is nonverbal. Mehrabian's research actually pertains to the relative importance of verbal and nonverbal messages during inconsistent communication. The real value of his work relates to communications regarding feelings and attitudes, for example in management and business, where motivation and attitude can have a significant impact on outcomes and results.[31]

Mehrabian found that **when communication is unclear—when the message and the delivery are inconsistent—we pay more attention to nonverbal cues to interpret meaning.** Many vocal and visual cues like voice, tone, facial expressions and body language are harder to control than words. This is likely a key reason that we intuitively pay more attention to nonverbal indicators when an individual's message and delivery are in conflict.

Our own communication experiences with people validate Mehrabian's findings. When the customer service representative answers your call with an annoyed tone and says they would be happy to help solve your problem, are you confident they will? When the industrial engineer says with a blank face and flat-line energy level that changes to the manufacturing process will improve quality and reduce rework by 10 percent, are you convinced? When your listeners compliment you with an awkward smile and minimal enthusiasm, do you believe them that you delivered an effective presentation? In each case, you are more likely to believe the individual's delivery signals over the words themselves.

This is especially true when the message being delivered is not a pleasant one. For example, if you are uncomfortable delivering a below-average performance review and have a tendency to smile or look away when nervous, you may give the impression that the situation is not as serious as it is. Your message is that performance needs to improve, but your body language says otherwise and leaves your employee questioning your message. Your employee may leave the meeting thinking they need to improve in a few areas, never understanding that their job is in jeopardy. In the end, the message you intended is not the message that was received.

One of my favorite quotes relating to communication is by Ralph Waldo Emerson: "What you do speaks so loudly that I cannot hear what you say." It highlights another way that our delivery can overshadow our message. Often our nonverbal behaviors are so strong or mismatched that they become a distraction from our message rather than an enhancement to it. When listeners are focused on what we are doing, we invite them to tune us out. If they aren't listening, we aren't building trust and don't have any hope of influencing them.

This reality hit home for me during a session with Lou Heckler, my speech coach. As we reviewed one of my video playbacks, we observed that my message and my

When it comes to message vs. delivery, delivery wins every time.

delivery were inconsistent. My coach rewound the video, muted the sound and had me watch it again. "This is what your listeners experience when your message and your delivery don't match," he said. "It's as if they are watching with the sound turned off. They see you but don't register what you are saying."

When it comes to message vs. delivery, delivery wins every time.

Think about that the next time you give a presentation, facilitate a team meeting or talk with a customer. If you are not consistent, your nonverbal behaviors will drive your message.

CONSISTENCY MAKES YOU RELEVANT

How many communication interactions do you think the average leader has each day, including email, text messages, phone calls, conversations and meetings? Fifty? One hundred? Several hundred?

In that kind of environment, how can you and your message be heard above the noise? What can you do to improve the chances of your phone calls being returned rather than ignored and your emails read instead of buried in an overstuffed inbox? How can you get people who are already busy to act on your recommendations when they walk away from your meeting or conversation?

The answer is to be consistent. **Consistency makes you relevant.** Few individuals are consistent in their communication. When your message and your delivery match–no matter how, when or where you communicate–you will stand out from the crowd and your message will stick.

In face-to-face interactions (where individuals can see each other, whether that be in person or virtually), all three communication pieces are present–verbal, visual and vocal. When those three are in sync, we build trust and create a standout experience for listeners that they will remember long after the interaction is over.

When we communicate via phone, we lose the visual element that exists with face-to-face. Without visual cues, our communication will be less influential if our message and vocal cues are not consistent. Think about phone conversations you have had where you hung up wondering, "Did I just offend her?" or "Did he really understand what I was trying to say?" Consistency eliminates doubt in our listeners' minds.

With any form of written communication, we have only one

element–words–to transfer our intended message and meaning. Written communication has the greatest potential for misunderstanding because the delivery cues are completely missing. With no visual or vocal signals, readers are often left questioning the intent and tone behind the message if our emails or text messages are poorly written.

Clients frequently contact us initially via email. Occasionally, my first impression has been that these particular individuals are going to be difficult to work with based on their email. When I meet them, my impression of them completely changes. They are positive, open, kind and responsive–quite different than the impression their emails convey. Think about the impact of an ineffective email if it is your first contact with a prospective customer or your only method of contact with an existing customer.

If email is problematic, texting and social media are even more so. Many of us struggle to get our point across face-to-face, much less to effectively communicate and be influential

Consistency eliminates doubt in our listeners' minds.

through a text or 140-character tweet. Because text messages and social media are used for quicker, more informal messages, we tend to get lazy when we use them, even in a business context. Have you ever received a text message that had so many misspellings or was so abbreviated that you had to send a message back asking the sender to break the code?

Communicating through email and text has become our norm. It's easy and saves time. It's where we are comfortable and confident, so we tend to hide behind the written words. Perhaps because the other person can't see us, we subconsciously think we don't have to put as much effort into our communication. With words as our only tool, how we write those words becomes paramount. Clarity as well as correct spelling, punctuation and basic grammar are essential. Being influential doesn't require you to be an English major or a professional writer. It does require you to pay attention to the details so that your communication is professional and consistent.

Clients often tell me, "When the communication is important, I spell-check and proof my writing." When I hear this excuse, my response is, "How do you know which written pieces are important?" Your name is attached to every message. **The email or text that is the most important is the one that makes the receiver question your knowledge, credibility or professionalism because it is unclear or filled with mistakes.**

For greater influence, hold yourself accountable to keep your messaging and your delivery consistent in every interaction, whether it be face-to-face, over the phone or by email or text. Treat every interaction as a high-stakes interaction. Don't fall into the trap of the "big gig." In every interaction, think beyond the message to your delivery. Focus not only on the words, but also on your voice inflection, gestures, body language and, yes, even spelling and grammar. No one can make that conscious effort for you.

Influence comes down to consistency—on both a micro and a macro level. At the micro level, influential leaders are consistent in their communication, earning the trust of their listeners. At a macro level, influential leaders authentically show up as the same person Monday to Monday®. That consistency builds a strong reputation that impacts their listeners before they ever say or write a word.

Treat every interaction as a high-stakes interaction—think beyond the message to your delivery.

What does your reputation say about you? Have you built a reputation that you are proud of Monday to Monday®? Find out in the next chapter.

SUMMARY

- Influence comes down to two different elements that often collide: what you communicate and how you communicate it.

- People are influenced by what you say *and* how you make them feel.

- When your message and your delivery are in conflict, your nonverbal behaviors drive the message.

- Being authentic, natural and letting your personality come through enhances your influence.

- Without trust, influence cannot occur.

- Influential communicators ensure that their message and delivery are consistent Monday to Monday®.

Take Action to Drive Your Influence to the Next Level

This is where the rubber meets the road. This is where you take what you learned about yourself in the self-awareness chapter and put it to use. Think back to the video you made of yourself speaking. (You did do that, right?) Now that you have a greater understanding of why consistency is so important, go back and review the playback four times (yes, four) using the following guidelines:

1. **Watch and listen.** Do you come across the way you want your listeners to perceive you, as trustworthy, credible and confident?

2. **Mute the sound and only watch your delivery.** Focus on your visual behavior. Are you fidgeting or over gesturing? Do you look like you have passion for your message?

3. **Unmute the sound but turn away from the recording and only listen.** Focus on your vocal behaviors. How do you sound? Do you use filler words? Do you pause and use brevity, or do you speak too quickly or ramble?

4. **Watch and listen again.** Are your messages and delivery consistent with each other? Do your facial expressions and body language match your message?

Write down the delivery behaviors that were inconsistent with your message. Commit to seeking feedback about how you can change those behaviors. Then practice every skill every day, one skill at a time.

CHAPTER 10

REPUTATION:

Who Are You, Monday to Monday®?

Your reputation enters the room before you do.

Several months ago, I received a call from a vice president of sales who had been referred to me by another client. "I need your help," he said.

"I hold a sales meeting with my team every Monday," he explained. "This last Monday, as I was walking down the hall toward the conference room, I overheard my team talking about me. Someone said, 'I wonder which Joe* is going to show up today?' A few people chuckled and then someone else said, 'Who knows? Your guess is as good as mine.'"

"That really caught me off guard," Joe admitted. "I had no idea my team felt that way. Even worse, I never realized that apparently I come across differently in different situations."

I pointed out to this vice president that he was actually quite lucky. Many leaders go through their entire careers never knowing what their teams are saying about them behind their backs. He had received the gift of feedback, albeit inadvertently and unexpectedly. Having heard the message loud and clear that he needed to improve his reputation, Joe was ready to change.

Have you ever known someone like Joe? A leader or colleague who

....

* Not his real name.

portrays themselves one way during meetings, acts differently in one-on-one conversations and seems different yet in emails and texts? You never know who you're going to get. Does it cause you to doubt their leadership or trustworthiness? Perhaps you know an individual who has a certain personality at work and an alter ego after hours. Do you question their credibility and authenticity? These individuals' inconsistent behavior minimizes the influence they have with you.

Consistency is a major factor in determining your level of influence. In the last chapter, I shared the importance of consistency between your message and your delivery. Now we want to look at consistency in a broader context, beyond your communication. In this chapter, I will share how your reputation impacts your influence and ask you to think about how you show up for every interaction, Monday to Monday®.

REPUTATION DRIVES INFLUENCE

Recently I was asked to coach the CEO of an advertising agency. The agency's board of directors brought me in because they believed she needed help with reputation management. She was known for being hard-core and rough around the edges. Her team felt she didn't listen to their ideas. Others perceived that she had an entitlement mentality and cared more about herself than her team. Bottom line, her organization did not respect her as a leader.

As I worked with her and gave her constructive feedback, she became defensive and exhibited the very behaviors I had heard about. The more strongly she reacted, the more calmly I responded. At the end of our first session, she said, "I need to learn how to handle challenging conversations like you do." I grinned, as this was exactly why her company had invested in her development. In the long run, she was not committed to changing, and her reputation continues to jeopardize both her influence and her success. It will be interesting to see how long the board keeps her as their CEO.

Your reputation determines your level of influence, shapes your relationships and drives the results you get from others. A negative reputation minimizes your influence whereas a consistently positive reputation enhances your influence. "Leaders with a negative reputation have to rely purely on their positional authority to influence their followers and others in the organization, which is typically not effective," shared Jon Finch, Vice President of Training and Recruiting at Milwaukee Tool. "A positive reputation helps you influence more efficiently."

Jon's insights from the business world are backed up with research. According to the Institute for Health and Human Potential (IHHP), "Most leaders don't realize that their reputation is an invisible force that shapes every decision that involves them: how people listen to them; how seriously others take their arguments, suggestions or ideas; and how fully people will commit to their vision and trust their direction."

"Your reputation either causes resistance and makes it harder for you to get things done–it causes people to avoid your phone calls and your emails–or it causes them to jump when you come up with an idea," explains Bill Benjamin, partner at IHHP.

Your reputation determines your level of influence, shapes your relationships and drives the results you get from others.

"A strong, positive reputation has an extraordinary effect on the amount of trust, credibility, respect, and ultimately on the influence you have with others. . . . This influence allows you to be more effective because you are able to do more with less and to do it with more speed, efficiency and support."[32]

Have you ever given thought to how your reputation impacts your influence? Do others seek out your advice and counsel? Do customers call you when they know you have a product or service they need? Does leadership come to you when there is an opportunity, special project or a promotion?

Perhaps Jeff Manby, Executive Vice President, General Merchandise Manager at Kohl's Department Stores says it best: "You are only as influential as your reputation."

DON'T LEAVE YOUR REPUTATION TO CHANCE

Your reputation is based on how people experience you, specifically your actions, behaviors and communication. Others create a perception of you based on what they hear and see you do. How do you treat those you work with? Do you respect your team members' time and efforts? Do you follow through on your commitments? Do you respond to others in a timely manner? Do you use a harsh or welcoming tone in your verbal communications? Are you professional in your emails, texts and social media posts? The answers to these types of questions give you a close look at your reputation.

Most of us would like to think we have a positive reputation, but how do we really know? As with our communication, we tend to get fake or faulty feedback about our reputation. I often tell clients, "Your reputation is what people are saying about you behind your back but not telling you to your face." If you have a negative reputation, people most likely aren't going to tell you.

Participants in our workshops frequently talk about their leaders' reputations. We hear about team leaders who routinely communicate clearly and concisely, as well as executives who consistently engage their audiences and hold their attention. Unfortunately, not all the leaders we hear about have positive reputations. One sales team shared that their leaders were constantly multitasking and consequently never gave their full attention to conversations, often leading to costly miscommunications. During another session when we were discussing interruptions, a participant said, "You know who could really use this training? Our CEO. He always interrupts people." How much influence do you think these leaders have with their teams?

Your reputation is who you are and how you show up, Monday to Monday®.

Have you ever considered what your peers, employees and customers may be saying about you behind your back? Do you know what kind of reputation you have? If you are missing that self-awareness of how people perceive you, positively or negatively, you are missing out on the opportunity to have a greater level of influence.

Many of us take our image and reputation for granted. Your reputation is not something you want to leave to chance. Give careful thought to the kind of reputation that you would be proud of Monday to Monday® and that would resonate with your purpose and priorities. This is what makes your reputation authentic. What do you want to be known for? What do you want people to think when someone says, "Hey, do you know [your name]?" These are critical questions that need deliberate answers. When you get clear about what you stand for, it is easy to be you Monday to Monday®.

Your reputation signifies how you define yourself and what others can expect from you. It is your promise, your personal brand. Your reputation is who you are and how you show up, Monday to Monday®.

"Your reputation is everything," says speaker and coach Lou Heckler. "People will long remember what you stand for when they have forgotten what you say."

YOUR REPUTATION ENTERS THE ROOM BEFORE YOU DO

Are there ever days when you look at your calendar, see *that* name next to a meeting and think, "Ugh, not today!" You know that meeting is going to run long because this individual is notoriously long winded and has trouble keeping the group on track. There is a good chance the group will have to meet again at a later date on the same topic. What kind of mindset would you have walking into that meeting? Perhaps you think, "I'll have plenty of time to catch up on email."

Now think about a leader who has a reputation for being a skilled facilitator and for getting things done. He or she runs productive meetings, is engaging and always concludes with clearly defined action steps. How do you feel when you see that individual's name on your calendar? Would you have a different mindset going into this individual's meeting compared to the one described above? More than likely, you would think the meeting will be worth your time.

Your reputation–good or bad–precedes you. Your reputation enters the room, your clients' offices, your meetings and your one-on-one conversations before you ever get there. The big question is, are you okay with that reputation?

"People will often form their opinion based on reputation before you get the chance to prove or disprove them. If your reputation is bad, you may not get the chance to prove them wrong," points out Phil Hildebrandt, Chief Executive Officer, Segall Bryant & Hamill.

Your reputation sets the stage for your interactions and their outcomes. A positive reputation predisposes your listeners to trust you, allowing you to influence them more easily. It earns you a certain level of respect from the outset. Your audiences show up with an open mind, a willingness to learn and a bias to accept your recommendations. A less-than-positive reputation predisposes listeners to question your credibility, knowledge, leadership and professionalism. You have to work that much harder to influence them.

"Your reputation as a leader increases or inhibits your ability to move the organization because of the group's preconceived notion of your capabilities," explains Jon Finch of Milwaukee Tool.

Your reputation precedes you with respect to written communication as well. Your reputation arrives in people's inboxes long before your emails do. Do you ever get an email and cringe before you open it based on the reputation of the person who sent it to you? A name alone can create a feeling or perception because it has a reputation attached to it. When you hear a name, you know what kind of experience you will have with that individual.

Eighteenth-century diplomat Charles Maurice de Talleyrand once said, "One's reputation is like a shadow. It is gigantic when it precedes you, and a pigmy in proportion when it follows." Always remember that your reputation arrives before you do. Make it work for you rather than against you.

CONSISTENCY BUILDS INFLUENCE

Think for a moment about companies that are masters at communicating their brand. They are successful because they are consistent. Take Starbucks for example. Walk into any Starbucks, order your coffee drink of choice, and it will taste the same whether you are in Paris, Texas, or Paris, France. What are your favorite brands? There is a good chance they are your favorites because you know what to expect from their product or service. They never leave you guessing.

These companies understand that consistency drives brand loyalty. Successful companies also know that brand loyalty is the key to getting people to buy into their next big idea or product. Think about companies like Google and Apple. People wait in line for days to be the first to own the latest iPhone or iPad. That is a prime example of how consistent branding drives influence and ultimately results.

Your personal brand is essentially the same as a corporate brand. **To be a trusted and followed leader, you need a positive, authentic and consistent reputation.** "Consistency is the only way to build a brand or reputation," says trust expert David Horsager.[33]

Your listeners and readers should never have to guess who is going to show up. They need to get the same *you*—the same personal brand— in every interaction. Are you just as engaging on a video call as you are presenting live to a group? If someone catches you in the hallway, are you still that attentive listener, no matter how busy you are that day? Are you as positive and passionate about the direction of the company when talking with your team as you are with the board of directors?

A solid reputation is built over time and requires a proven track record. You can't establish a track record if a different *you* shows up on different days or in different circumstances. When your actions, behaviors and communication are inconsistent, you create a reputation for being unreliable and possibly untrustworthy. You may become known as someone who is insincere or disingenuous, someone who turns "it" on or off depending on the circumstances. Others will second-guess you, your recommendations and your leadership.

Influence is built by consistently living your personal brand Monday to Monday®. "Every day, through every communication and interaction you have, every room you walk into, every hand you shake, every picture you post, blog you publish, comment you make, tweet, 'Like' or Facebook posting you make, you are sculpting your brand," says success guru Darren Hardy.[34]

Influence is built by consistently living your personal brand Monday to Monday®.

Clients often say to me, "When I'm on the phone or texting with someone, it's a more relaxed situation. Why can't I be more informal?" This is the kind of thinking that sabotages their influence. Communicating with influence doesn't mean being stiff or overly formal. It means being authentically you in every interaction, no matter whom you communicate with and no matter what medium you communicate through. It is when you try to be someone you're not that you get into trouble. If you "fake it" in high-stakes situations by being more formal than you naturally are, you won't be able to maintain that personal brand Monday to Monday®.

This is also when I want to wipe clean people's thinking that key presentations or meetings are the end-all be-all and other interactions really aren't that important. When you are authentically you Monday to Monday®, you will be just as effective and influential in the daily interactions as in the "big gigs." That is when your influence will begin to grow dramatically.

I have talked a lot in this book about being influential Monday to Monday®. Notice that I don't talk about being influential from 9:00 to 5:00, Monday to Friday. That is because **influence is a 24/7/365 endeavor**. Your reputation and your influence need to be constantly nurtured and maintained. You may be unfailingly consistent with your words and actions Monday through Friday. If you then do something over the weekend that is out of sync with your brand, you will undermine all your efforts.

Consistency predicts the conversations others have about you behind your back. How you show up in every interaction builds your reputation. The more consistent you are, the faster your positive reputation will grow and spread.

IT ONLY TAKES SECONDS TO DESTROY WHAT IT TOOK YEARS TO BUILD

Nothing can kill a reputation and influence faster than inconsistency. Just one small slip can change others' perception of you and permanently damage your reputation.

In a previous organization where I worked, there was a leader who was very well regarded. This individual always spoke highly of his team, especially in group situations. One day, he apparently wrote an email bashing a team member that he had just raved about in a meeting. He accidentally sent that email to more than one person, including the person he was bashing. Big mistake! That one misstep destroyed his credibility, jeopardized his influence and impacted his ability to lead his team.

Any exception can undo the reputation you have built: a poorly worded text, an indiscreet conversation, a "little white lie," an action that is perceived as hypocritical. Billionaire businessman and philanthropist Warren Buffett wisely stated, "It takes twenty years to build a reputation and five minutes to ruin it. If you think about that, you'll do things differently."[35]

My speech coach Lou Heckler once gave me a piece of advice that a friend had given him years ago: "You are always under surveillance." At the time, Lou's friend didn't mean it literally. His point was that people are always watching us and, right or wrong, forming opinions based on what we say and do. In today's world, when just about everyone has a camera and video recorder on their phone, these words of wisdom take on a whole new meaning.

Today's world is all access, all the time. **You are always on display, and your reputation is always on the line.** Your actions can be recorded, even without your knowledge. Case in point, the CEO of a major corporation who was caught on an elevator surveillance camera repeatedly kicking a dog. After the video was released online and thousands of people pledged to boycott the company's products, he was forced to resign.[36]

Nowhere is the chance to damage your reputation more likely than with social media. Social media is an incredible tool, allowing us to share a message instantly with thousands of people with just a few keystrokes. That communication has the potential to be seen by more people, faster, than at any other time in the history of mankind. That is the good news . . . and the bad news. Social media is also the riskiest medium because of the high probability of miscommunication and unintended negative connotations. The more social media channels you use, the greater the risk of damaging your reputation.

Social media amplifies and broadcasts our human mistakes. Who among us hasn't botched a joke or made an ill-timed, inappropriate comment? How many of us face lifetime consequences for it? When a single post can go viral in a matter of hours and be read by millions of people around the world, we must be vigilant. Once a post is out there, it is likely captured forever.

It seems not a week goes by that we don't hear about some politician, celebrity, sports figure, business leader or "average Joe" who has gotten themselves into hot water over something they posted on social media or something they did that was captured on social media. Consider these true stories of individuals whose lack of consistency had disastrous consequences for their reputations and careers:

- A director of corporate communications tweeted what she thought was an innocuous comment to her 170 followers. Then she turned off her phone for an eleven-hour transcontinental flight. By the time she landed, her post–which was perceived as racist by most who viewed it–was the number one worldwide trend on Twitter. Within weeks, she was fired and her career was ruined.[37]
- A man sitting at a tech industry conference leaned over and privately shared a joke that just popped into his head with a friend. A

woman sitting in the row in front of them overheard the joke and felt it was indicative of the gender issues plaguing their industry. She turned around, snapped their picture and tweeted it out to her nine thousand followers with a post calling the men out. Two days later, the man (a father of three) was fired from his job.[38]

These examples show painfully well how easily a reputation can be destroyed in seconds due to one bad move. Once you've damaged your reputation, you've also damaged your credibility, trustworthiness and influence. Repairing a damaged reputation is challenging because people tend to remember the negative more easily and longer than the positive. In an article titled "Bad Is Stronger Than Good," Florida State University social psychology professor Roy Baumeister and his colleagues state: "Bad impressions . . . are quicker to form and more resistant to disconfirmation than good ones."[39] Your reputation, credibility and influence are difficult to regain once lost.

The above examples also show how the lines between our work and personal lives have blurred, if not been erased completely. **What you do and say and post in your personal time absolutely impacts your professional life.** It bears repeating one more time: maintaining your reputation and influence is a 24/7/365 job.

The ancient Greek philosopher and scientist Aristotle reportedly said, "We are what we repeatedly do. Excellence, then, is not an act but a habit." Being consistent creates influential habits. You will position yourself in the top 1 percent of all leaders and be well on your way to being more influential if you will discipline yourself to be authentically consistent Monday to Monday®.

Now that you understand the importance of self-awareness, consistency and reputation in growing your influence, you are ready to take on the next element in the model: adaptability. Influential communicators have the ability to adapt their message and style to their audiences' needs and expectations. Let's find out how they do it.

SUMMARY

- Your reputation sets the stage for your interactions and their outcomes, determines your level of influence, and drives the results you get from others.

- Reputation is based on how people experience you, specifically your actions, behaviors and communication.

- Give careful thought to the kind of reputation that you would be proud of Monday to Monday® and that would resonate with your purpose and priorities.

- Your reputation precedes you. A positive reputation predisposes your listeners to trust you, allowing you to influence them more easily.

- Influence is built by consistently living your personal brand Monday to Monday®. Your listeners and readers need to get the same "you" in every interaction.

- Maintaining your reputation and influence is a 24/7/365 job. One small slip in consistency can permanently damage your reputation and your influence.

Take Action to Drive Your Influence to the Next Level

Today, commit to building and maintaining the reputation you want for yourself by doing the following:

1. List two to three adjectives that describe how you want to be perceived by others.

2. Ask a few individuals to tell you one word that describes how they perceive you. Does that word match one of the adjectives you wrote down above?

3. Before you walk out the door each morning, look in the mirror. What kind of first impression will you make? Do you represent the personal brand you described above? If not, make the change needed to be consistent.

4. Write down three action steps you can take to grow your personal brand and show up consistently Monday to Monday®.

5. This week, check all your social media profiles to ensure they are aligned with your personal brand and promote a positive reputation.

YOU MAY NOT BE AS INFLUENTIAL AS YOU THINK YOU ARE IF . . .
You are the only one talking during a meeting.

Have you ever gone into a meeting (either physical or virtual) intending to do a "data dump"—to share as much information with as many people as quickly as possible? Do you ever feel awkward facilitating a meeting because you don't know how to get participants to interact? The discomfort of silence convinces you to do all of the talking just to "get it over with." Without listener interaction you have no idea what your listeners' needs are, what questions they have, and if they understand and agree. Communicating a message that focuses only on you, your objectives and your expectations is not likely to influence others.

Your natural response to this situation might be to—

1. Continue talking without pauses to avoid interruptions, questions or awkward silences
2. Talk faster to get through the meeting or call as quickly as possible
3. Make the assumption that your listeners are following and understanding your message

For Influence Monday to Monday®:

1. **Set up the session.** At the beginning of the meeting, tell your listeners that you will be moving through the material quickly to honor their time. Then explain that you will ask questions throughout the session to ensure they are receiving the value they expect.
2. **Speak in short, clear and concise sentences.** Few things are harder to follow than a leader who is vague in defining goals, decisions and direction. Communicating clearly and concisely may seem obvious, but it is far easier said than done.
3. **Pause at key intervals to check for understanding.** When you complete a key point, take a "pulse check" by asking, "What questions do you have about . . . ?"
4. **Invite interaction by asking open-ended questions.** For example: "What are your thoughts on . . . ?" "What experiences have you had with . . . ?" Then make certain you pause to give listeners time to respond.
5. **Make a connection.** Only speak when you see your listeners' eyes. This will also allow you to continuously read your listeners so you can adapt your message on the fly to meet their expectations.

FEEDBACK

PRACTICE

INFLUENCE

IMPACT

ADAPTABILITY

REPUTATION

CONSISTENCY

SELF-AWARENESS

ACCOUNTABILITY

CHAPTER 11

ADAPTABILITY:

Focus Outward Rather Than Inward

Adapt your message on the fly without skipping a beat.

I learned about the importance of adaptability the hard way.

For many years, Stacey Hanke, Inc. was honored to partner with a major pharmaceutical company, regularly training its team members how to communicate with influence. The first several years, every group was composed of enthusiastic salespeople. They were like sponges, anxious to learn how growing their influence would lead to more sales.

Without realizing it, I started to get too comfortable and lazy. I began showing up to sessions without doing my homework, assuming that every group we worked with at this company would be equally energized and talkative. That was my first mistake.

This assumption hit me in the face the next time I walked into their corporate training room. The participants entering the room that day looked as if they were walking into an IRS audit (no offense to IRS agents out there). As I approached them before the session to chat, they were quiet, hesitant, unsure why they were there. Rather than adapting my style to match their demeanor, I opened my presentation with the same level of energy that had always worked in the past. Mistake number two.

Overlooking the possibility that a different group might be sitting in front of me, I didn't ask any initial questions that might have provided some insight into who these participants were and what they wanted to get out of the training. Instead, I proceeded with my planned A-to-Z presentation. Mistake number three.

I was clueless when I began giving sales examples, only to discover that these participants were from the financial department. The room quickly turned on me. My faulty assumptions built a wall between my listeners and me. I was communicating that I didn't care about was important to them because I hadn't taken the time to get to know my listeners. I damaged my credibility by not adapting my message and delivery to meet their needs and objectives. It took much of the day to regain some respect and trust from this group.

These missteps seem so obvious, especially for a seasoned presenter. You might even think there is no way you would make the same mistakes. I repeatedly observe leaders diminish their influence because they don't understand their audience and adapt their message accordingly. Engineers and research and development teams talk over their listeners' heads and get caught up in details that only an engineer could get excited about. Creatives who believe their work sells itself fail to clearly explain why they chose the design elements they did and how those choices meet the client's objectives. Lawyers and financial and human resource professionals who often communicate with acronyms and technical jargon leave their listeners wondering, "What does that mean?"

The solution to these influence challenges is to become a master at adapting your message to your audience. The first step is to *know* your audience so you can personalize both your message and your delivery to meet their needs.

(Note: The elements of influence we have discussed to this point have been primarily focused on you, the communicator. In this chapter, we will focus on the listeners and readers you communicate with. For ease and simplicity, I will use the word "audience" to collectively refer to the listeners and readers who receive your messages.)

START WITH "WHY"

"Influence is getting people to take the action you want them to take, because they want to take it." That was the answer I got from Sam Zakhem, Program Manager with the U.S. Army Corps of Engineers, when I asked him his definition of influence. Sam nailed it on the head. In order for action to take place, you typically need to change your listeners' or readers' opinion, knowledge, attitude or behavior. They will change when they have a compelling reason, what I call their "why."

In their best-selling book *Made to Stick: Why Some Ideas Survive and Others Die*, authors Chip and Dan Heath discuss the six traits of "sticky" ideas and messages. One of the six traits of sticky messages is that they are emotional. They give your audience a reason to care about your idea. "For people to take action, they have to care," say the authors. " . . . it's not about pushing people's emotional buttons, like some movie tear-jerker. Rather, the goal of making a message 'emotional' is to make people care. Feelings inspire people to act."[40] In other words, sticky messages tap into the audience's "why."

Your audience's "why" should be at the core of every message you communicate.

How often do you think about your audience's "why"? If you are like most busy leaders, you begin a message (either verbal or written) by thinking about what you are going to communicate and how you will communicate it. Before you ever open your mouth, laptop, email app or smart phone, you need to identify the "why":

- Why is your topic important to this particular audience?
- Why is this conversation or interaction happening now?
- Why should they take the action you want them to take (i.e., how will it benefit them)?

Your audiences' "why" should be at the core of every message you communicate. Although this might seem like common sense, many leaders think they can communicate the same message to different audiences and achieve comparable results. This is often not the case.

For example, do you or your team repurpose proposals for prospective clients, using the same boilerplate language and changing only the client name and the product/service offerings and cost? Think about how much more effective those proposals might be if you specifically acknowledged each client's "why" and how your products/services address it. Do you send standard thank-you notes to clients after completing a project? Imagine the impact of tailoring those thank yous to the client's future objectives and how you can help them meet those objectives by continuing to work together.

One message does not fit all. If you are a CEO planning to communicate one annual speech to the entire organization, your words may fall on deaf ears. Each individual will hear your message from a different perspective and with varying levels of knowledge and experience. Key takeaways for frontline team members will be different than for senior leadership. Each team will need to hear something meaningful to them in order to buy in to your vision. What is important to sales and marketing might not be relevant to operations. Information critical to finance may be immaterial to human resources. For the greatest influence, identify each team's why and adapt your message to each.

Sales professionals often ask me, "What can I do? My customers are just not interested in our other products." Similarly, clients will say, "The information I need to share is boring. People just aren't interested." Have you ever found yourself thinking or saying statements like these? If so, this is your wake-up call!

Your product or service, your topic and your audience are not the problem. There is no such thing as a boring topic—only a boring message or a boring communicator. As difficult as this may be to hear, you need to know the truth. The problem is likely that you and your message are not interesting because you do not understand your audiences' "why." As a result, they tune you out. **Your message will gain traction if you let your audiences know what is in it for them.** When they personally connect with your message, they are more likely to change. Adapt your communication to them, and they will never lose interest in what you have to say.

K.N.O.W. YOUR AUDIENCE

Years ago, before I began working in the communication industry, I was a leader with a large manufacturing company. Every quarter, the CFO gave a financial update to the leaders. She showed slide after slide, each one so crammed full of figures we had to squint to even try to read them, and state the obvious: "I know you can't read this, but . . ." Then she went ahead and tortured us anyway. It was all about the numbers. I used to look around the room to see if others were as disconnected as I was. Some people were having side conversations, some were buried in their technical gadgets catching up on email, others were staring off into space, and a few were getting in their nap for the day.

The CFO might have been an effective communicator in a room full of financial analysts, but she missed the mark with us. She didn't know her audience. She assumed we understood what she was talking about and never attempted to interact with or engage us. She was essentially having a conversation with herself. As a result, her message didn't stick, and she lacked any influence with us.

Nancy Duarte is an expert in presentation design and the CEO of Duarte Design, the largest design firm in Silicon Valley. She is well known for her TED talks and best-selling books, including her latest, *Illuminate: Ignite Change Through Speeches, Stories, Ceremonies, and Symbols.* When asked by TED Blog about the keys to a great presentation, she shared, "The number one thing, I think, is to be audience-centric. To take the time to think through who the audience is and develop all your material from a place of empathy toward them. You're asking them to adopt your idea, which means they may have to abandon a belief they hold as true—and that's hard. Know your audience—take a walk in their shoes. What keeps them up at night? How are they wired to resist your message?"[41]

Nancy's advice to know your audience applies to any kind of verbal or written communication, not just presentations. Understanding your audiences' why is a good start, but it's not enough. You need to gain an even deeper understanding of your audience. To do that, I recommend a tool called K.N.O.W.–an acronym that allows you to quickly and easily personalize your message:

Knowledge–What does your audience know about your topic, and what language will resonate with them? Although you may have a wealth of knowledge about a subject, your audience doesn't need to hear everything you know. Avoid wasting precious time communicating irrelevant details or information your audience is already familiar with. Use language your audience will clearly understand. Avoid talking over your audience's heads and using industry-specific terminology.

Need–What does your audience need to know in the amount of time you have with them in order to take the action you want them to take? Asking this question is an extremely effective time management tool that forces you to pare your message down to the most essential information. How often do you find yourself in a situation where you wish you had sixty minutes to communicate your message, but you are only given thirty? One of the worst things you can do as a communicator is to speak longer than your allotted time or to write unnecessarily long emails or texts. It sends the message that you don't respect your listeners' and readers' time and negatively impacts your reputation.

Opinion–What is your audience's opinion about your topic? How will they likely respond to your information? What preconceived notions might they have? What has been their experience with you, your product or your company? The answers to these questions will help you prepare for potential objections, questions or concerns your audience may have. When you address these up front, you communicate to your audience that you sincerely care about what is important to them.

Who–Who specifically is your audience (e.g., board members, employees, customers, etc.)? What other information do you need to consider or find out that will help you tailor your message to them? Who needs to be included in the communication? Have you ever gone to a meeting only to discover that the decision maker wasn't present? Or perhaps you've been copied on an email that didn't pertain to you. Hone your influence by ensuring the right players–and only the right players–are included in your communication.

K.N.O.W. can be used to personalize any message through any medium: sales calls, meetings, conference calls, webinars, face-to-face conversations with a coworker or boss, voicemail messages, emails, texts and even social media posts. (If you are preparing for a high-stakes presentation, download a free, comprehensive listener analysis at www.InfluenceRedefined.com. Complete the analysis before you begin developing your message.) If you are unsure of the answer to any of the K.N.O.W. questions, try to find out the answer beforehand or start the interaction with a few targeted questions.

K.N.O.W. is like a communication GPS that will help you successfully navigate through any interaction. **When you adapt your message to each audience using their words, emotions and level of understanding, you position your ideas in a way your audience will respond to and connect with.** The more personalized your message, the faster you build trust, credibility and influence.

PREPARATION GOES A LONG WAY

"When I'm prepared, I'm a better communicator." This is one of the most common reasons people give to explain why they don't communicate as effectively as they would like to. Perhaps you have thought the same thing. It is absolutely true. Preparation is crucial. As the wise adage states, "If you fail to prepare, you prepare to fail." Your audience is less forgiving when they can tell you haven't prepared (like my audience of financial professionals I told you about at the beginning of this chapter). To achieve influence Monday to Monday®, **prepare for every interaction ahead of time whenever possible**.

I bet I know what you are thinking. I know because it is one of the biggest complaints we hear from our clients: "Stacey, I don't have time to prepare!" Almost every leader I work with is overworked and overscheduled.

The good news is that **you can think about your audience's "why" and run through the K.N.O.W. acronym in about five minutes**. Investing just five minutes to prepare for those important meetings, phone calls, emails and social media posts actually saves you time in the long run. Attention expert and thought leader Neen James points out, "You have to invest time to save time. When you invest the time to adapt your message for your audience, you save time by eliminating confusion and not having to explain your message again. Plus, it's a great way to hold your audience's attention."

The majority of our daily interactions are impromptu. We spend our days sprinting from one email, text or conversation to the next. To be influential leaders, we need to effectively communicate off the cuff. How can we possibly prepare for those spur-of-the-moment interactions? Again, the solution is K.N.O.W.

You can quickly go through K.N.O.W. in your mind while driving to your appointment, dashing to the next meeting, or while the phone is still ringing after you see who is calling. Even if you only have a minute, you can consider the most critical questions: What is your audience's "why"? What do they **Know** about your topic? What information do they **Need** to take the action you want them to take? What is their **Opinion** on your topic? **Who** are they?

With a little practice, you can consistently communicate with confidence, credibility and influence even during impromptu interactions. The time you take to apply K.N.O.W. ensures your message will meet their expectations. **A few minutes of intentional preparation will go a long way with your audience.**

Which Medium Will Influence the Most?

How many of us are guilty of emailing or texting back and forth with someone when we could pick up the phone or walk down the hall and reach a conclusion in a matter of minutes? We rationalize that this is a more efficient way to communicate, but is it *effective*? Does it hinder or help our influence?

A key component of adaptability is choosing the communication medium that will have the most influence based on your message and audience. When you are intentional about which medium you push your message through, you make it easy for others to respond to you and increase the likelihood they will take action.

Ask those with whom you communicate frequently (e.g., clients, colleagues and team members) which communication medium they prefer. Then do your best to accommodate them. I have some clients who want me to communicate with them via text to grab their attention. If I didn't know this was their preference, I would waste time and energy sending emails or leaving voicemails without ever getting a response.

Keep in mind that even if an individual tells you they prefer written communication, there will always be times when a phone call or face-to-face meeting is most effective. Case in point: introductions. When you have the opportunity, meet in person. You don't want to leave that first impression up to chance. Other examples: when you have disappointing news to deliver, when you are asking someone to take on added responsibility, or if there is any chance you could be misinterpreted.

Before you hit send on your next email or text message, ask yourself, "Is this the most effective medium to influence my audience?" Adapt your medium to your audience and watch your influence grow.

ADAPT ON THE FLY WITHOUT SKIPPING A BEAT

Golf is a challenging game. (Any golfers reading that statement are smiling and thinking, "No kidding!") Not only are you competing against other players, but also against the course itself. Because every course and every hole are different, you have to adapt on the spot. You choose different clubs, change your approach and adjust your swing depending on varying factors: the weather, course conditions and obstacles, the length and layout of each fairway, and how far you are from the hole. You have to read the green and determine which way the ball will break. The most successful golfers are those who have the strongest core skills and are the best at adapting their game.

Communicating with influence is a lot like playing golf. Although you use the same foundational influence and communication skills in every interaction, you have to constantly adapt your message and delivery to the specifics of the situation. Even when you know your audience and show up fully prepared with a plan, circumstances can–and usually do–change. You have to be able to read your audience and adapt.

- You might be involved in an email exchange with the leader of another department when you realize your reader doesn't have the level of knowledge you thought they had about the topic. You need to adjust to give them more background information and then ask questions to confirm their understanding.
- You are giving a presentation and can see by the glow of phone screens around the room that your audience is losing interest. Instead of talking louder and faster to grab their attention, you can change your energy level and re-engage the group with a story, analogy or example tailored to the situation.
- You discover that your customer previously had a bad experience with your product/service, and you had no idea prior to the meeting. Switch gears and address their disappointment. Clearly state what you and your company will do to guarantee their experience with your product/service is positive going forward.

"It's important to be attuned to the listener's needs. Too many people just plow forward without regard to their audience," explains Mark Gale, CEO of Charleston|Orwig. "Even with preparation, it's sometimes necessary to radically change a presentation or discussion to fit the needs and expectations of the audience."

Another difference between good communicators and influential leaders is that **influential leaders have the ability to adapt their message and delivery seamlessly in the middle of an interaction**. Here are four steps to adapting your message on the fly:

1. **Be present.** When I ask clients how they define executive presence, many immediately say, "Someone who is present." Then they confess that being present and focused is one of the most challenging aspects of communicating with influence because it requires consistent, conscious effort. We often don't pay attention to what we are saying and doing, much less what our listeners are saying and doing. Being present means being completely focused on your audience and fully in tune with what is happening between you in the moment.

   - Do you need to adjust your energy level based on the energy and mood in the room?
   - Are you talking nonstop, or are you pausing to give your audience a chance to absorb your message?
   - Are you typing an email to one client while you're on the phone with another?

2. **Observe.** I often see leaders who are so caught up in their message that they don't see what is happening right in front of them. Pay close attention to the verbal and nonverbal signals your audience is sending that indicate you need to adapt your message or delivery. Read your audiences' body language:

   - Are they interacting with you, or have they tuned out and are checking their technical gadgets?

- Do they need additional information, or do they have that blank stare that indicates you've given them too much?
- Do they truly understand what you are telling them, or are they nodding their heads "yes" in the hopes you will wrap it up soon?
- Are your email/text recipients only answering some of your questions because your messages are so voluminous they become overwhelming?

3. **Interact to understand**. Check in with your audience and seek feedback by asking open-ended questions that will guide you in personalizing your message and knowing what adjustments to make. Dig deeper with questions such as—
   - *What are your thoughts on . . . ?*
   - *What has been your experience with . . . ?*
   - *What was your takeaway from our conversation?* (If your listeners miss the key takeaway, you know you have more work to do to communicate messages that are heard, understood and acted upon.)

4. **Listen (and read) beyond the words**. Remember that what your audience says is often different than what is really going on. Consider hidden agendas. For example, is budget really an issue, or have you not adequately communicated the value of your product/service? Is lack of resources the real reason they are questioning your idea, or are they not clear about your objectives?

Learning to change your message on the fly without skipping a beat based on what you hear and observe in the moment takes practice and focus. It is one of the most difficult steps to growing your influence. This is why we covered the importance of feedback, practice and accountability early in the book. Communicating with influence is a commitment, but one that is worth the effort.

Do you ever feel like for every one interaction you have there are actually three: the one you prepare, the one you actually have and the one you wish you'd had? That is a sure sign you need to be more adaptable. Adapting your message on the fly to meet your audience's needs prevents those "I wish I'd said/written" regrets.

GET OUT OF YOUR HEAD

I once coached a CEO who never left the podium when he spoke. Even with a clicker in hand, he was glued to the spot, and he followed his slide deck so closely that he couldn't carry on a natural conversation.

"Why don't you ever leave the podium?" I asked him one day.

"Well, I have to operate my slide deck," he answered.

"Why do you need to operate your slide deck?" I asked.

"Because all my points are on the deck. I can't present without my deck." As soon as he said it, he grinned. He knew where I was going with this. "I need to make sure that all the information on the slides gets communicated and heard," he continued as if to validate his reason. "I'm concerned I'll forget what to say."

How adaptable do you think this leader was? Do you think his messages resonated with his audiences?

In many communication situations, we are our own greatest obstacle to influence. We think we must stick to our plan no matter what. We focus on our own agenda or simply getting through the interaction. Our fears and negative self-talk take control, and we break out the "What ifs." *What if I adapt my message, and it's not well received? What if I change something, and it doesn't work? What if I don't know what to say? What if I forget what to say? What if I say something wrong?*

I understand these concerns because I used to have them myself. Early in my speaking career, I wrote out my presentations word for word and spent hours memorizing each speech. My boss at the time, whom I both loved and hated because he was always right, shared this wisdom: "Stacey, if you keep memorizing those speeches, there will come a day when you are standing up on that stage and you'll forget and won't be able to find your place." I should have listened to him. One day my memorization technique failed. I just stood there with that dreadful deer-in-the-headlights look on my face.

I got smart. (Or so I thought!) I started writing my key points on index cards. The next time my boss saw me present he said, "Stacey, someday your nerves are going to take control, and you will drop the cards." Again, I ignored his wisdom. I will never forget the day he proved me wrong. I was giving a speech to hundreds of people, and in the middle of my presentation, I dropped the stack of cards. I watched in horror as they scattered below me. I couldn't talk without my cheat notes. I began frantically shuffling the cards with my foot under the podium as if no one could see me. Clueless! Can you imagine what my audience thought? I was far from influencing anyone.

Have you ever gotten caught up in the beliefs and self-talk in your head? Adaptability goes out the window when you are trapped in your internal dialogue and wedded to your prepared plan. Here are some tips to help you avoid getting caught up in your own dialogue:

- **Stay in the moment.** Avoid the temptation to get ahead of yourself. Avoid thinking about the next item on your agenda or bullet on your slide. Instead, stay focused on what you and your listeners are saying. If someone asks a question, resist the urge to immediately start thinking of your answer before they finish talking. You run the risk of not hearing the question correctly, missing what is important to your listener and providing an inadequate response.
- **Cut, don't cram.** Have you ever been speaking in a meeting or giving a presentation and suddenly realized you had only five more minutes of time and fifteen more minutes of material? Did you think to yourself, "I can talk fast"? Rather than eliminate information, we try to cram ten minutes' worth of content

into five minutes. The more you cram, the more you confuse. Your listeners only know what you tell them and show them. Your audience doesn't know you have three more key points and won't notice if you cut them. Use your remaining time wisely to connect with your audience's why and to give them only the information they need to take action.

- **Accept responsibility for communicating clearly.** A sales representative once told me a story about a sales call he made with his manager. Rather than using the brand name of his product in talking with the customer, the rep used an in-house acronym. Observing what was happening, the sales manager asked the customer if she knew what the acronym meant. She replied, "No." The sales rep had assumed the customer understood because she had been nodding her head throughout the conversation. This example brings up the question of who is responsible for a miscommunication—the communicator or the listener/reader. The answer is always the communicator. Your audience should not have to work to understand your message. As the communicator, you need to do the work. Rather than blame someone for misunderstanding, accept responsibility for miscommunicating. Always check for understanding by asking, "What questions, thoughts or concerns do you have?"

- **Focus outward rather than inward.** Too often our focus is on ourselves and what we want to communicate rather than on our listeners and readers and what they need. If you're focused on yourself, it's difficult to find common ground with your audience. Your listeners can tell it's all about you and what you want to accomplish. If you are not focused on what is important to them, why should they trust you? Why should they act on what you have to say? Take the focus off yourself, and put your energy into how you can help your audience solve a problem or make a change. Have a two-way interaction with your audience rather than giving them a monologue.

When you are adaptable and focused on your audience, you never have to worry about the "what ifs." If your self-talk starts to take over, refocus on your audience by asking, "What does my audience need to know in the time I have left with them?" Trust your competence. You will have the answer and then you will know what to say. With practice, you will get to a point where you can confidently think on your feet no matter what conversation you are having.

The next time you get ready to communicate a message, consider this: Your audience is the most important aspect of your message. **You need your audience more than they need you.** You need them to do something–take action, change their opinion, buy, invest, give discretionary effort, spread the word. The message is not about you and what you want to accomplish. It is about your audience.

Influential leaders never think about what they can get. They focus on what they can provide, establishing a real connection and relationship that leads to impact beyond the interaction. We will discover the importance of impact, the final element in our influence model, in the next chapter.

SUMMARY

- Influence is getting people to take the action you want them to take, because they want to take it.
- Adapting your message and delivery to the specifics of the situation allows you to consistently communicate with confidence, credibility and influence, even during impromptu interactions.
- Messages that resonate tap into the audience's "why."
- K.N.O.W. your audience to quickly and easily personalize your message.
- Prepare for every interaction ahead of time whenever possible.
- When you are adaptable and focused on your audience, you never have to worry about the "what ifs."

Take Action to Drive Your Influence to the Next Level

Identify a work-related topic you will be communicating this week, such as facilitating a meeting, delivering a presentation, having a face-to-face or virtual conversation, writing a report or preparing a proposal. Practice adapting your message and see for yourself how it increases your influence.

1. Find your audience's "why":
    - Why is your topic important to this particular audience?
    - Why is this conversation or interaction happening now?
    - Why should they take the action you want them to take?
2. Create a message that resonates by identifying your listeners, K.N.O.W.:
    - What do they **Know** about your topic?
    - What do your listeners **Need** to know in the amount of time you have with them in order to take the action you want them to take?
    - What is your listeners' **Opinion** about your topic?
    - **Who** specifically are your listeners?

3. Adapt your message on the fly without skipping a beat:
    - Be present.
    - Observe.
    - Interact to understand.
    - Listen beyond the words.

4. Avoid getting caught up in your own dialogue:
    - Stay in the moment.
    - Cut, don't cram.
    - Accept responsibility for communicating clearly.
    - Focus outward rather than inward.

CHAPTER 12

IMPACT:

Influence Beyond the Interaction

It's not only about how you show up, but what you leave behind.

Krystal was already a successful pharmaceutical sales representative when I began coaching her. She was frustrated because she had recently taken a job with a new company and been thrown into a sales territory that had been neglected for some time. Despite her best efforts, she was having difficulties getting the doctors in her territory to consider her company's drugs for their patients.

As with most industries today, pharmaceutical sales is highly competitive. Salespeople spend their days going from one office to another, hoping for a precious few minutes to convince a distracted doctor that their company's drugs are better than the competition's. Like most salespeople in similar situations, Krystal crammed as much of her message as possible in what little time she had with each doctor (two to three minutes on a good day). She never knew when she might get face time with them again, so she talked . . . and talked fast.

I shared with Krystal that she was spending valuable time talking to doctors but not inviting them to share their patients' needs. I suggested she talk less and listen more. She was skeptical based on the success she'd had in the past. "Why would I let the doctors do most of the talking when I'm the one with the knowledge and expertise about our products?"

Krystal had the same false assumption that many salespeople, leaders and other professionals have: They tend to think that because they know their products/services, solutions, visions or goals better than anyone, they should do most of the talking. Our clients frequently share their concerns that if they don't communicate everything they know, their listeners won't perceive them as knowledgeable.

Krystal finally agreed to try my suggestions. I coached her to K.N.O.W. each doctor before the sales call, to ask open-ended questions and actively listen to the doctors' responses, and then adapt her message accordingly. I shared how she could have greater impact by creating a memorable experience for her clients that would allow her to stand out in the crowd of pharma reps.

A few months later, she called with an update: "You were right. Letting the doctors do more talking helps me understand their needs and their patients' needs and promote the right solutions. I realize now my old approach was like throwing darts at a dart board that didn't even exist, hoping something would hit the mark. This is so much easier . . . not to mention more effective!"

If you are thinking this story simply illustrates a good sales strategy . . . you are right. The reason this sales strategy, or any sales strategy, works is *influence*! You can have the best sales technique in the world, but if you lack influence, your results will never be as good as they could be. Good technique and experience will always be trumped by an unclear message, distracting delivery behaviors or a less-than-positive reputation.

Not only did Krystal learn to adapt her message to her audience, she also began to have a lasting impact on her clients. As she gained influence with the doctors, they were more willing to see her and often spent more time with her. "Now doctors are prescribing my drugs more consistently and continuously, rather than being convinced to switch to a competitor's drug by the next rep that walks in the door," she told me.

"I've also noticed that doctors are now more willing to try a drug from my company that they haven't used in the past."

You probably won't be surprised to learn that Krystal's sales increased, as did her success. When she started the new job, she was ranked sixty fifth out of sixty five reps in the western US region. Within two years, she was ranked number one of 130 sales reps nationally.

This is a powerful example of influence, even if you are not in pharmaceutical sales. No matter your industry or position, it is harder than ever to get on people's calendars. Yours is just one of many meetings, calls or emails vying for their time and attention. When you do get their attention, you have precious few minutes to share your message. Your opportunities to influence others are shrinking at a time when it takes longer to build relationships and earn trust. It is more difficult than ever to be heard, let alone be memorable. This is precisely why being influential Monday to Monday® is so critical.

If you have followed the action steps I have laid out in this book, you have gained influence. Through self-awareness, consistency, managing your reputation and adapting your message to your audience, you are communicating with greater influence and achieving better results in your interactions.

What happens when your interactions are over? Does your influence continue? Are you able to move people to action even when you are not physically present?

Impact is the final element of influence. It is the key to achieving enduring influence and sustained results.

INFLUENCE³—MOVING PEOPLE TO ACTION LONG AFTER THE INTERACTION

Many leaders mistakenly believe that having influence in the moment is enough to ensure results. This is why the current influence paradigm focuses on only having influence during critical events such as high-stakes meetings, crucial presentations or key sales calls.

With the demands of today's business climate, you need influence that lasts beyond the moment. Every interaction has to have a greater return on your investment of time, energy and effort. You want to move people to action both during and long after an interaction. I refer to this as **Influence[3]–moving people to action three days, three weeks, three months, even three years after an interaction**.

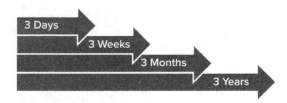

Influence[3] = Moving People to Action Long After the Interaction

True influence is enduring, and it is exactly the kind of influence you need for sustained results in the business world. Influence[3] keeps the board, executive committee and organization committed to following your vision. Influence[3] is how you get consistent, discretionary effort from team members. Influence[3] is the way to retain customers in a competitive market. Influence[3] is what compels a prospect you long forgot about to pick up the phone and contact you.

About five years ago, I met an individual at a conference where I was the keynote speaker. After my presentation he introduced himself. "I am the CEO of a new credit union that is small but growing. I would love to bring your organization in to train my people, but we don't have a budget for training. I need time to work with my board to prove my capabilities before I can make a case for training." I focused our conversation that day on his long-term goals for his team and shared some resources to help him resolve his immediate needs.

The same CEO recently contacted me to say that he is now in a position to hire my company to train his team how to communicate with influence. I have not had a conversation with him in over five years. This is Influence³.

How do you achieve this kind of lasting influence? Start by looking at every interaction through a wider lens. Ask questions such as—

- **What is important beyond today and this interaction?** Focus on long-term goals and objectives, both yours and your audience's.
- **What value can you bring to the interaction?** In our busy lives, the last thing you want is a reputation for wasting people's time by not delivering value and purpose in every interaction.
- **What can you do and say to build a long-term relationship?** Concentrate on developing a relationship rather than initiating a transaction.

For every presentation you give, every conversation you have, every email or text you send, every social media post you make–think about what you can do to influence beyond that moment. When you do that, you will see even greater results than what you are now achieving.

CREATE A STANDOUT EXPERIENCE THAT IS UNIQUE AND MEMORABLE

Influence³ is based on an experience between you and your audience. What you leave behind is determined by how you make people feel. **Creating a positive, standout experience enables you to command the attention of any audience and leave a lasting impression.**

Do you know a doctor who has a terrific bedside manner? Think for a moment about how that doctor communicates and makes you feel. Now think about a doctor whose bedside manner is lacking. Do your interactions with this doctor feel different than those with the first?

> *What you leave behind is determined by how you make people feel.*

Chances are you feel that the doctor with the excellent bedside manner cares more about you and your health. He or she created an experience with you that stands out more vividly in your mind than your interactions with other doctors. When you come across someone who truly connects and engages with you–particularly in today's busy world–that individual is memorable. More than likely, the doctor with the engaging bedside manner has more impact and influence on you.

It is no coincidence that some of the most influential leaders of our time are masters at creating a standout experience. Have you ever experienced provocative thought leader Daniel Pink, groundbreaking researcher Brené Brown, world-renowned orchestral conductor and leadership expert Benjamin Zander, or creativity expert Sir Ken Robinson? There is a reason their TED talks have been seen millions of times and are some of the most viewed in the world. I encourage you to watch these influencers in action at Ted.com. You can learn a great deal from observing others. Experience for yourself how they make their message stick and leave a lasting impression long after their presentations are over.

Do you create a standout experience that keeps your listeners and readers engaged? What kind of lasting impression do you make? Is it something unique and memorable, or the same experience they get from everyone else?

Many business professionals believe that what makes them stand out is being an excellent speaker, an effective communicator or a dynamic leader. The truth is that these are simply the minimum standards for doing business today. Excellent speakers, effective communicators and dynamic leaders are a dime a dozen. If you possess one or even all of those characteristics, what you think makes you better or unique really only makes you the same as everyone else.

Creating a standout experience is a set of learned skills and behaviors. You will separate yourself from the crowd when others consistently perceive you as trustworthy, credible, confident, knowledgeable, authentic and passionate (the six key characteristics of influential individuals). Each Element of Influence that we have explored builds these skills, behaviors and characteristics and contributes to a standout experience:

- Self-awareness–Are you aware of the perception you leave with your listener after every conversation?
- Consistency–Are your message and delivery consistent with each other?
- Reputation–Are you consistent Monday to Monday® in every interaction?
- Adaptability–Are your message and delivery tailored to your audience's needs?

Impact is the final piece of the influence puzzle. **Impact allows you and your message to be heard above the noise and leave a lasting impression you are proud of.** You can create a memorable, standout experience by connecting with your audience, practicing brevity, leveraging the power of the pause and sharing your passion. Let's look at each of these in detail.

MAKE A CONNECTION

I have four beautiful nieces that I cherish spending time with. I confess that on occasion I may not give them my full attention. When that happens, my three-year-old niece, Sienna, will not so subtly bring me back to present by grabbing my face in her little hands and turning it so that I am looking directly in her big blue eyes. Her older sister, Jayla, will implore me with her big heart, "Auntie, talk to us with your eyes."

Children inherently understand the importance of real connection. In this technological age, too many adults have forgotten how to genuinely connect with one another. No matter how often we may "connect" with others through email, text or social media, nothing compares to an authentic, in-person connection.

Eye connection is a powerful way to build trust, develop relationships, have impact and create a standout experience with listeners. This is not a spelling error. I mean eye *connection* rather than eye *contact*. We have been taught for years to make eye contact when speaking with someone. We were told to look at everyone when speaking to more than two individuals by scanning the group or audience.

Eye connection goes beyond eye contact. **Eye connection is looking at an individual in the eyes and being 100 percent focused on that person for a full sentence.** When speaking in a group—

Eye connection is the primary delivery skill that builds trust.

even to a large audience—you continue eye connection by looking at one individual in the eyes for a full sentence before moving on to look at the next person in the eyes for a full sentence. You only speak when you see eyes. No eyes, no talk. (Now that's tweetable!) Once you try eye connection, you will understand the huge difference between scanning and connecting for a full sentence.

Eye connection is the primary delivery skill that builds trust. Scanning your listeners or looking away mid-sentence (as with eye contact) creates the perception that you are untrustworthy. Maintaining eye connection signals to listeners that you are 100 percent focused on them and their needs. When you are focused with your eyes, you are focused in your thoughts.

Eye contact invites your listeners to disconnect and do anything but listen to you. Eye connection is an incredibly effective tool for engaging your listeners and holding their attention. Even in a large group, you can quickly and authentically connect with many individuals in a short time. A gentleman came up to me once after I gave a keynote to a large audience. "I have a bone to pick with you," he said with a grin on his face. "I came to your session thinking I could catch up on my email."

Not knowing what he was going to throw my way next, I asked, "What happened?"

"I knew you could see me. I wasn't going to let you catch me on my phone."

When you make eye connection with individuals, you personally engage them. It's as if you are having a one-on-one conversation with each person, no matter how large or small the group is. Your listeners are more likely to be engaged from start to finish, because they don't want to run the risk of you catching them on their device, having a side conversation or not paying attention.

Cassandra Farr, Region Leader of Florida for GE Healthcare, set a personal goal to engage her listeners through eye connection. Her efforts have paid off. "Team members tell me they appreciate that I'm connecting with them and paying attention to them. They feel that they are being heard and that I am truly listening to them, which is the best feedback I could receive as a leader."

Eye connection is a skill that requires discipline to learn. If at first you are uncomfortable with eye connection, keep pushing through the discomfort. Remember, if you're comfortable you're not growing. Like the other influence skills, eye connection will become habit with practice.

One of the most common pieces of feedback we receive after conducting corporate training workshops or keynotes is: "Our leaders never stay off their technical gadgets this long. What are you doing to keep their attention?"

We smile and say, "We are connecting with them."

MORE ≠ BETTER

When it comes to our communication, many people believe that the more we say or write, the more knowledgeable and credible our listeners and readers will think we are. In most cases, the opposite is true. **The more we speak or write, the more we confuse and frustrate our audiences.**

Research by Dr. Paul King, Chair of the Communication Studies Department at Texas Christian University, revealed that listeners experience what he calls "anxiety in listening performance." King found that the longer a speaker talks, the more listeners feel they need to remember, creating anxiety. The more listeners feel they need to remember, the more pressure their brains take on, creating a backlog of information that causes the brain to fatigue and tune out.[42]

Brevity creates greater impact.

Communicating too much information invites our listeners and readers to shut down and disengage. Although it may seem counterintuitive, brevity creates greater impact. Communication expert Carmine Gallo makes a powerful point: "What isn't there makes what is there even stronger."

Sid Chapon, Executive Vice President of Leadership and Organizational Development for global advertising agency Leo Burnett, is a coaching client who has learned the value of brevity. "Many leaders believe they need to share a lot of information with an audience to prove their knowledge. I've realized that communicating a few key messages concisely and accurately has more impact. I've also noticed that I am able to capture the attention of my audience faster and keep them engaged longer."

Kristin Derwinski, Director of Organizational Development at Briggs & Stratton, echoes those sentiments. "As leaders grow in their careers, some of their biggest communication challenges are brevity and clarity," she shared. "As you move from a manager role to the director and vice president levels, you have to shift from sharing the details to providing the executive summary. As the size of your 'stage' grows, communicating a simple and clear message becomes critical."

You can make your message more impactful by practicing brevity:

- **Ditch the details.** Share only the information that is necessary to achieve the desired results. Avoid getting bogged down with details that aren't relevant (especially in text messages). Listeners and readers want a clear, to-the-point message without any fluff.
- **Stick to three or fewer key points.** Research like Dr. King's shows that giving less information actually increases the amount of

information your listeners and readers remember. When you commit to "less is more," your audience is more likely to take action.

- **Prepare, think and speak/write in bullet points.** Most of the individuals I observe speak in run-on sentences–which lead into paragraphs–causing them to ramble and take forever to get to the point. Use bullet points when preparing speaking notes to trigger your thoughts and help you stay on track. Bullet points are also easier for your listeners and readers to follow, digest, remember and act on.

Never underestimate the power of a clear and concise message. Your listeners and readers don't have time to wait for you to get to the point . . . and neither do you.

THE POWER OF THE PAUSE

Have you ever noticed that great comedians pause after delivering the punch line to a joke? The pause is where the experience lies for the audience. It gives listeners a chance to understand the joke and respond. Imagine if comedians never paused. The audience would miss the next joke because they would still be thinking and laughing about the last one. It wouldn't take long for them to become frustrated, and that is no laughing matter.

The same concept holds true in communication. Non-stop talking and run-on writing creates frustration for listeners and readers. They crave moments of silence to catch up and let your message sink in. Pausing gives listeners the chance to hear, process and internalize your message. The more they understand, the more likely they are to act.

Non-stop talking is one of the biggest communication mistakes I observe. When most people find themselves rambling (and that is if they are self-aware enough to notice), they continue talking, torturing their listeners even more. They believe *if* they keep talking, eventually they will get to their point.

A few well-positioned moments of silence resonate with listeners. Silence is uncomfortable for those who don't know how to leverage its power. For greater impact and influence, we need to get comfortable with silence. Publilius Syrus said, "I have never regretted my silence. I have regretted my speech."

Often times we are uncomfortable pausing because our subconscious lies to us, telling us that if we pause, our listeners will think we don't know what to say. We also mistakenly believe that if we pause, others will interrupt us. Multiple clients have shared their concern that in their corporate culture, if someone stops speaking for even a moment, people will try to steal the floor.

Pausing gives listeners the chance to hear, process and internalize your message.

We need to change these misperceptions. **The reason we get interrupted is not because we pause, but because we *don't* pause.** We are interrupted when we take too long to get to the point or when our listeners can't get a word in edgewise.

Having the self-awareness and discipline to stop talking and pause is a powerful communication and influence skill. Not only does it benefit your audience, it puts you in control of the situation, what you want to say and how you are going to say it for greater impact. Pausing sends the message that you are confident and self-assured. Leveraging the power of the pause also allows you to—

- **Adapt your message.** The pause is where adaptability occurs. When you stop talking, you give your listeners the opportunity to ask questions and share their ideas, opening a dialogue that gives you insights into their needs and expectations. Pausing allows you to focus on what is happening in the moment so you can adapt your message on the fly without skipping a beat.
- **Practice brevity.** Become aware of when you are saying too much. Then pause to gather your thoughts, refocus your message, take a relaxing breath and give your listeners time to catch up.

- **Eliminate filler words.** Whether I am working with executives, sales representatives or other professionals, I find that filler words are often the first word spoken and typically continue throughout the message. *Actually, okay, you know, like, basically, and* and *but* are common filler words. The word *so* is especially prevalent. "So I want to talk to you about . . ." Filler words undermine your credibility. The solution? Replace filler words with a pause.
- **Get back on track.** When we forget what to say, our subconscious screams, "You forgot, and everyone knows it!" Our typical reaction is to use filler words to hide the fact that we forgot and to give us time to think on our feet. Using filler words immediately communicates to listeners that we don't know what to say. If you forget, stop talking! Trust your competence. Give yourself permission to think, and the words will come to you.

Pausing is crucial in written communication as well as spoken. Have you ever received a lengthy email that was one continuous paragraph? Frustrating, isn't it? The start of a new paragraph is similar to a pause while speaking. It signals the reader that you have completed a thought and are transitioning to another topic. You can even use a *pause* in a text message. Rather than one long, arduous text, hit the return key to create space between thoughts or topics.

The pause is where adaptability occurs.

Pausing requires more focus than most people realize. My clients consistently confess how surprised they are at how difficult it is to learn to pause. When they experience the many benefits of pausing, they admit they would never go back to using fillers.

PASSION PERSUADES

Have you ever had one of those moments when you were "on fire" as a communicator—when people were hanging on your every word and you knew you were rocking it? I bet you were passionate about your

topic. Influential leaders are not afraid to show their passion because
they understand that **communicating with passion engages and persuades listeners**.

For his book *Talk Like TED*, communication expert Carmine Gallo
analyzed five hundred of the best TED Talks and identified the common elements that are scientifically proven to increase the likelihood a
pitch or presentation will be successful. Passion is one of those elements. "You cannot inspire others unless you are inspired yourself,"
Gallo says. "You stand a much greater chance of persuading and inspiring your listeners if you express an enthusiastic, passionate, and meaningful connection to your topic."[43]

> Passion is contagious and
> moves people to action.

When we coach leaders to communicate with passion, they often
express concern: "If I show passion, I won't be perceived as professional
or serious." Speaking with passion is not having over-the-top energy
and smiling ear to ear. It starts with genuinely and whole-heartedly
believing that your message will help your audience in some way and
then authentically transferring that belief to your audience.

Influential communicators tap into their emotions and put their
heart and soul into both their message and delivery. Sharing a compelling personal story that ties to your topic is an effective way to add passion and make your message stick. You can show passion in your delivery
through purposeful gestures, tone, volume and facial expressions.

"Passion is both authentic and charismatic," says author and speaking coach Nick Morgan. "We don't fully trust people until we've seen
them get emotional . . . because these moments allow us to take the
measure of their values."[44]

Passion is contagious. It pulls listeners to the edge of their seat and
leaves them wanting more. It keeps them talking about you and your
message long after the interaction is over. Passion creates a memorable,
standout experience that moves people to action.

MAKE AN IMPACT, LEAVE AN IMPRESSION

A great deal of creating impact in your communication is overcoming the lies your subconscious tells you. You have to continuously fight that voice that tells you to scan the audience rather than connect individually, to give your audience more information rather than less, to keep talking rather than pause, and that being professional is more important than being passionate.

When you connect, practice brevity, pause and show passion, you set yourself apart and leave a lasting impression. Think about the leaders you interact with. Do they use all of these impact skills or only one or two? Few individuals communicate with impact so when someone does, you remember it.

You will know you have made an impact on your audience by how they respond to you. They will be attentive rather than distracted by their technical gadgets. They will be actively engaged, asking questions and dialoguing with you on a deeper level. They will trust that what you are recommending is the right choice for them and that they are in the right hands. They will promptly reply to your phone calls, emails and texts. They will engage with you through social media.

In the long-term, your relationships will have more meaning and depth. The trust that your customers, colleagues and team members have in you and your capabilities will grow. When individuals reconnect with you, they will still refer to the experience they had with you. At some point in the future, they will think of you when they—

- Want to partner with a reliable and trusted resource
- Have the budget to purchase the products you sell
- Join a new company and need the services you offer
- Need to hire or promote someone

Effective leaders can achieve results in the moment. Influential leaders achieve results Monday to Monday® and beyond.

SUMMARY

- Impact is the key to achieving the enduring influence and sustained results necessary for success in today's business world.

- For every presentation you give, every conversation you have, every email or text you send, every social media post you make, think about what you can do to create influence three days, three weeks, three months, three years after the interaction.

- Creating a positive, standout experience allows you and your message to be heard above the noise and leaves a lasting impression.

- Eye connection—looking at an individual in the eyes and being 100 percent focused on that person for a full sentence—is the key to building trust.

- Practice brevity by communicating a clear, concise message.

- Pausing gives listeners the chance to hear, process and internalize your message and puts you in control of the situation.

- Passion engages and persuades listeners.

Take Action to Drive Your Influence to the Next Level

It's time for an accountability check. At the end of the chapter on self-awareness, I challenged you to video and audio record yourself. Have you done that yet? If not, what are you waiting for? You owe it to yourself to video record yourself this week. As you view the playback, watch for the influence skills we discussed in this chapter:

- Do you connect with your eyes or scan your listeners?

- Is your message clear and concise? What words can you eliminate that clutter your language?

- Where could you add pauses for greater impact?

- Do you communicate passion about your topic? If you were a participant in this conversation, would you believe and trust your message?

- Do you create a standout experience for your audience?

- What kind of lasting impression do you make?

YOU MAY NOT BE AS INFLUENTIAL AS YOU THINK YOU ARE IF . . .
Customers aren't buying from you like they used to.

Your products and services practically sold themselves in the past. You and your company pride yourselves on having a solid reputation and strong relationships with your customers. Yet you've noticed that your customers don't call you anymore when they have a problem your products and services could help them solve. Times have changed. As competition has increased, so have customers' buying options.

Your natural response to this situation might be to—

- Over-sell, offering customers numerous options in the hopes that one will be the right fit
- Take over control of sales conversations, creating customer frustration and confusion
- Offer customers *your* solution, regardless of whether it addresses their pain points

For Influence Monday to Monday®—

1. **Stop talking and start listening**. If you are not actively listening to your customers' pain points, you risk offering the wrong solution, losing your customer's trust and jeopardizing the relationship. Be patient and avoid the temptation to hijack the conversation. An influential communicator understands the power of speaking less and listening more to discern what the customer really wants and needs.

2. **Ask influential questions.** Focus on asking open-ended questions that identify your customer's pain points. Open-ended questions will give you more information about what is important to your customer and their objectives.

3. **Adapt your message on the fly.** Be flexible and willing to allow your customer's responses to drive the direction of your message.

INFLUENCE

IMPACT

ADAPTABILITY

REPUTATION

CONSISTENCY

SELF-AWARENESS

FEEDBACK

PRACTICE

ACCOUNTABILITY

THE POWER OF INFLUENCE

Grow your influence and become the leader
you were meant to be, Monday to Monday®.

Congratulations! You have reached the pinnacle of the Influence Model. If you completed the action steps at the end of each chapter, you have gained self-awareness. You have discovered the importance of consistency between your message and your delivery and in the daily actions that determine your reputation. You have learned how to adapt your message on the fly and how to leave a lasting impact on your audiences. You are well on your way to enhancing your influence and becoming the leader you were meant to be.

This is not the end of your influence journey. It is only the beginning. **Communicating with influence is an ongoing process.** There is never an end to the Influence Model. The arrows form a continuous loop because you need to constantly seek meaningful feedback, practice daily and hold yourself accountable. We seem to readily accept the notion that if a professional athlete were to lose commitment, reject coaching and stop practicing, we would see a decline in performance. We don't accept the same principle when it comes to our own performance and results. The truth is, if you don't use it, you lose it.

Gaining influence can sometimes be a two-steps-forward, one-step-back process. You may hit it out of the park by adapting your message on the fly in a presentation, only to find yourself rambling and fidgeting in a conversation the next day. You might eliminate "um" and "ah" from your vocabulary only to start using the filler word "right" or "so." Having setbacks along your influence journey is part of the process. Instead of throwing in the towel when you get off course, check in with your accountability partner. Go back to the three drivers (feedback, practice, accountability) and diligently follow the model. Before long, you'll be back on track. Influence has a steep learning curve. Once you become aware of your bad habits, you can correct them faster.

Being influential Monday to Monday® requires stamina, discipline and focus. Achieving anything of value or significance rarely comes easy. If communicating with influence Monday to Monday® were easy, everyone would be influential, but they're not.

Every summer I have the honor of speaking to financial professionals enrolled in a three-year management program at Pomona College in Claremont, California. I spend a day with the year-two students teaching them the how-tos of influence. Walking the campus last summer, I was approached by an individual who had participated in my presentation the prior year. "Stacey, I attended your session last year and found it so valuable," the woman said with excitement. "You shared so many practical skills and techniques. It was great . . . but I can't do it."

I listened as she dropped the *can't* bomb several times in the sentences that followed. It was like a blown-up balloon slowly, sadly losing its air.

When she finally paused, I jumped at the chance. "You're right, you can't."

Her eyes grew to the size of saucers. "What do you mean?"

"It sounds like you have already convinced yourself that you can't communicate with influence," I said. "Imagine where you would be today if you had put your energy into practicing the skills and techniques we discussed last year, rather than convincing yourself you can't do them."

This was the wake-up call she needed. Several months later, I received an email from her. "Thank you for telling me what I needed to hear," she wrote. "After our conversation, I made the decision to stop making excuses and commit to putting my energy into enhancing my influence skills. I'm proud to say I've received positive feedback from others on how my confidence and credibility have increased."

Either you believe you can communicate with influence, or you believe you can't. Either way, you're right.

I believe you can grow your influence and become the leader you were meant to be. I know you can. I've coached thousands of leaders, and every single one had the potential to become more influential and a more effective leader. Not all of them were willing to do the work.

Individuals who are influential Monday to Monday® are disciplined and committed to doing the work of an influencer. They are committed to practicing, asking for feedback and learning from their mistakes. They live by the motto: The most difficult things to accomplish in our lives have the greatest personal and professional investment.

Personal development expert Jim Rohn once said, "If you want to have more, you have to become more. Go to work on yourself harder than you do on your job. Success is something you attract by the person you become."[45]

I have given you everything you need to know to grow your influence, as well as the tools and resources to do it. The question is, **now that you know what to do, are you willing to make the commitment to do the work?**

The goal of this book has never been to help you gain greater influence simply for influence's sake. Rather, the goal has always been to help you gain greater influence to make lasting change in your career, your team and your organization. Let's see what that might look like.

THE POWER OF INFLUENCE IN YOUR CAREER

Having greater influence will have a significant, positive impact on your career no matter your role, profession or industry.

I once presented the topic of communicating with influence at an international animal healthcare conference. Afterward, a veterinarian came up to speak to me. "I never thought that influence was something I needed to focus on in my business," he shared. "I take care of dogs, cats and small animals. During your session, it dawned on me that I should be having more conversations with the animals' owners. The more I communicate with influence, the more confidence they will have in my diagnosis and the more they will trust that I'm the right person to take care of their pets. I realize now that I've been missing a big opportunity to grow my business."

Cassandra Farr, Region Leader of Florida for GE Healthcare, also discovered that communicating with influence can have a profound impact on one's career. "I took on the challenge to create a seven-year, multi-layer contract package for one of our most important clients. This was a highly complex project that had never been attempted before. People told me it would never happen.

"I had to work with every function in every product area in our business," Cassandra explained. "Because I had learned how to communicate with influence and had practiced extensively, my communication was very clear about the benefits for our customer and our business. With greater influence, I was able to keep the team focused on the end goal, and we were able to get the contract done. As a result, I was promoted and won a major award."

Leaders who are influential Monday to Monday® create a ripple effect. Phil Hildebrandt, Chief Executive Officer of Segall Bryant & Hamill, used this analogy: "If you drop a stone in a pond, you'll see the rings in the water flow out. This is what true influence looks like. Your sphere of influence gets bigger as those people you influence in turn influence even more people."

Matt Church is the founder of Thought Leaders Global and author of eight leadership books. He was recently named one of the top ten motivational speakers in the world. Matt was one of

> *Leaders who are influential Monday to Monday® create a ripple effect.*

my coaches. He helps thought leaders capture, package and deliver what they know in a way that allows them to be more successful.

Matt's personal influence has led to the creation of a community of thought leaders positioned across the planet. By sharing their expertise, each of these thought leaders is having a lasting impact on the people within their community. That is the power of individual influence. One man's influence led to thought leaders, which led to positive changes within communities worldwide.

Influential leaders multiply their influence. The most impactful speakers of our time had immense and enduring influence on our world: John F. Kennedy, Martin Luther King Jr., and Mahatma Gandhi. Impactful business leaders such as Zig Ziglar, Steve Jobs and Estée Lauder, to name just a few, have had lasting influence.

John C. Maxwell, one of the world's top leadership experts, says, "The greater the impact you want to make, the greater your influence needs to be." **What could you personally achieve with more influence?**

THE POWER OF INFLUENCE WITH YOUR TEAM

Nothing gets accomplished without the ability to influence others to act on what you have to say. Becoming an influential leader raises employee morale, strengthens team dynamics, improves productivity and decreases time spent clarifying miscommunications. Without influence, your team will not follow you. Without followers, your day-to-day responsibilities become difficult to achieve.

Your team is only as strong as your level of influence. "The ripple of influence—or lack thereof—is felt throughout a team and organization," says Mark LeBlanc, founder of Small Business Success and my business coach. "People have a deep desire to follow a leader who inspires them to be their best. A leader's level of influence determines whether employees will go the extra mile or stop short of reaching their potential. Influential leaders have a greater likelihood of inspiring people to move mountains."

Your influence determines how your team behaves, how they interact with each other and how they interact with clients. I can usually gauge how much influence a leader has by the way his or her team members interact with me and with one another in a workshop or presentation. My observations almost always match what I find when I meet the leader. The influence of the leader is reflected in the team.

Influencing your team starts with modeling the behavior you want others to emulate. If you want individuals on your team to have greater influence, it begins with you. You must hold yourself accountable before you can hold your team accountable.

The influence of the leader is reflected in the team.

Not long ago, I spoke at an organization's global conference. As I sat with their leadership team in the front row watching the CEO present, the CFO next to me was on her technical device checking email during his entire presentation. When it was her turn to speak, she encouraged participants to focus on their development and to not check email while they were in conference sessions. Many of her team members heard her say one thing but saw her do the opposite.

The camera is always on. Your team is always watching.

I recommend to the executives and senior leaders of our client organizations that they be the first to practice and apply the influence skills we teach if they want their teams to follow. It is probably no surprise to you that some ignore my advice. In training sessions, their team members often ask, "Why do I need to communicate with influence when our leaders don't?"

Even when team members don't voice these frustrations, the lack of leadership influence quickly becomes apparent. One CEO who chose not to learn how to communicate with influence asked to close our training session with his leaders. This CEO's communication and influence skills had many opportunities for improvement. I observed that his leaders (who had just spent two days with us learning the how-tos of influence) now saw him in a new, less-than-positive light.

"The most critical action a senior leader can take to boost their organization's ability to communicate with influence is demonstration," says Shontra Powell, Vice President of Global Solutions for Johnson Controls. "Show your team what is expected and how it's done. This trickles down and sets a culture tone."

You can't expect others to be better if you're not willing to commit to being better first. One of the most powerful ways you can lead your team is by learning the skills of influence and modeling them for your team. Rosabeth Moss Kanter, Harvard Business School professor and Director of the Harvard University Advanced Leadership Initiative, once said, "Leaders are more powerful role models when they learn than when they teach."

Influential leaders are known for the positive, personal impact they create, one follower at a time. **What does your team say about your leadership? What are you known for?**

THE POWER OF INFLUENCE WITH YOUR ORGANIZATION

As your influence as a leader grows, so does your ability—and responsibility—to drive organizational change.

"Leadership is about vision, and it takes influence to get people to buy into that vision, empower them and produce change," shared Jill Tomalin, Chief Operations Officer of Credit Union National

As your influence as a leader grows, so does your ability—and responsibility—to drive organizational change.

Association. "Influence takes an organization into the future. Having influence allows you to exploit opportunities; not having influence often means missing out on opportunities."

Jon Finch, Vice President of Training and Recruiting at Milwaukee Tool, echoes those sentiments. "Influential leaders garner support and create movement within the organization. When leaders use their influence to positively affect the people around them, the health of the organization increases. The opposite is also true—when leaders cannot or do not communicate effectively, the organization will make decisions away from growth and health."

Being an influential leader does not always involve getting others to act on a positive recommendation or to make a positive change. **The true test of a leader's influence is during challenging times.** Influential communicators are able to move others to consistently give the discretionary effort that makes an impact, in good times and in bad.

I recently worked one-on-one with a leader at a Fortune 500 company. She received a promotion during a time of significant change and layoffs within the company. Not surprisingly, employee morale was low, which had impacted productivity. A key aspect of my client's new job was to communicate to her team why these difficult changes and layoffs were necessary, while also earning their trust as their new leader. A tall order!

We adapted her weekly messages to ensure they resonated with her team's concerns and needs. I pointed out the importance of presence. Any time she interacted with her team, she needed to exude confidence in herself, her plan and the company. She practiced to make sure her words and delivery were consistent. If her message and her body language had been out of sync, her team would have questioned her belief in her plan and leadership.

She ran with my recommendations and is seeing the benefits in the positive relationships she is building with her team. Her boss recently told her, "This is the leader we wanted in this position."

I have been selling influence and communication skills training and coaching for more than a decade. No one is going to invest time and money to bring my company in if they don't believe they will receive real value and results from our training. If I hadn't been influential in selling our services and cultivating client relationships, I would be out of business. The fact that my company has experienced steady growth over the last decade, even when many companies cut their training budgets, is a testament to the principles of influence.

From the boardroom to the hallway, from the sales meeting to the annual meeting, your level of influence drives your results.

What if every employee in your organization had the power to build relationships? How much stronger would your company culture be?

What if you could hold your clients' full attention all the time, every time? How much more business would you win and how much better would your results be?

What if your presence was as powerful as your business instincts? How much more effective could your leadership be?

IF NOT NOW . . . WHEN?

Once a year, I present to the freshmen and sophomores at the University of Chicago on the topic of influence. After one session, a young man came up and thanked me, sharing his takeaways from the presentation. As he left, he stopped, turned to me and said, "Someday I want to learn to communicate influentially."

"Why not today?" I asked.

"I'm not ready yet," was his reply.

John Addison is former co-CEO of Primerica and co-author of *Real Leadership: 9 Simple Practices for Leading and Living with Purpose.* In his book, John explains, "Most people live in the land of someday."[46]

This is true with many of the individuals we train and coach. *Someday* they will have time to focus on their development. *Someday* they will hire a coach to improve their executive presence. *Someday* they will learn to communicate with influence. Before they know it, they've run out of somedays.

We often follow up with participants thirty days after coaching. One of the questions we ask is which influence skills have been working for them. Many answer, "I haven't had a chance to practice."

I'm blown away when people tell me they haven't had a chance to practice. They haven't had one conversation in thirty days? (Every interaction is an opportunity to practice the skills of influence.)

Developing yourself as an influential leader isn't about having the time. There will never be a day when you say, "I have a week with nothing to do. I can now focus on my development." If you've been neglecting *you*, why not make yourself a priority?

Addison concludes, "Greatness doesn't happen in a day, or a week. It's the result of growth and maturation, and that can only happen over the course of time and committed constancy."[47]

Your choices dictate your level of success. Communicating with influence is no different. It requires commitment and discipline. It is all about the choices you make. Only you can determine the level of influence you will have.

If you only read this book and do nothing to implement the action steps, your communication will look and sound the same a year from now as it does today. Without a commitment to take action, you will be no more influential than you are right now. Are you okay with that?

What if you made a commitment to video or audio record yourself and watch/listen to the playback at least once a month?

What if you chose to step outside of your comfort zone by asking someone you trust to tell you how others really perceive you when you communicate?

What if you chose to ignore the internal voice that tells you if change doesn't feel comfortable, you're not going to do it?

What if you let go of your ego and asked daily for real, constructive feedback on your communication skills?

What if you chose to practice daily and be conscious in the moment during every interaction?

What if you made the commitment to find and regularly meet with an accountability partner?

What if you stopped the excuses and decided to invest in yourself?

What if you chose just one thing to increase your level of influence and created an action plan to make it happen?

Imagine what kind of leader you could be one year from now if you made those choices.

Take action today. Not tomorrow, not next week, not someday in the future when the time happens to be right. If not now, when?

Make your someday today and become the leader you were meant to be Monday to Monday®.

RESOURCES TO GROW YOUR INFLUENCE

Stacey Hanke, Inc. Blog: http://www.staceyhankeinc.com/blog/

Stacey Hanke, Inc. LinkedIn: http://www.linkedin.com/in/
staceyhanke

Stacey Hanke, Inc. Twitter: https://twitter.com/StaceyHankeInc

Stacey Hanke, Inc. YouTube: http://www.youtube.com/staceyhanke

Take 5® One Year Online Mentoring Program: http://www.
staceyhankeinc.com/take-5/

For tools presented throughout the book: www.InfluenceRedefined.com

RECOMMENDED READING

Talk Like Ted: The 9 Public-Speaking Secrets of the World's Top Minds by Carmine Gallo

The Naked Presenter: Delivering Powerful Presentations With or Without Slides (Voices That Matter) by Garr Reynolds

The Trust Edge: How Top Leaders Gain Faster Results, Deeper Relationships and a Stronger Bottom Line by David Horsager

Resonate: Present Visual Stories that Transform Audiences by Nancy Duarte

Essentialism: The Disciplined Pursuit of Less by Greg McKeown

Made to Stick by Chip Heath and Dan Heath

The Power of Full Engagement by Jim Loehr and Tony Schwartz

What Got You Here Won't Get You There: How Successful People Get More Successful by Marshall Goldsmith

Blink: The Power of Thinking Without Thinking by Malcolm Gladwell

Enchantment: The Art of Changing Hearts, Minds and Actions by Guy Kawasaki

Success Magazine: http://www.successmagazine.com/

TEDTalks Business (podcast): http://www.podbean.com/podcast-detail?pid=135138

ENDNOTES

ARE YOU AS INFLUENTIAL AS YOU THINK YOU ARE?

1 "Anything You Can Do . . . " *The Economist*. The Economist Newspaper, 11 Mar. 2014. Web. 04 June 2016.

CHAPTER 1

2 Maxwell, John. *21 Irrefutable Laws of Leadership*. N.p.: Thomas Nelson, 2004. 13. Print.

3 Al-Greene, Bob. "Did You Know 144.8 Billion Emails Are Sent Every Day?" *Mashable*. November 27, 2012. Accessed September 30, 2014. http://mashable.com/2012/11/27/email-stats-infographic/.

4 Radicati, Sara, and Quoc Hoang. *Email Statistics Report*, 2011–2015. Palo Alto: Radicati Group, 2011. Print.

5 *Heywire Business*. "Business Text Messaging: Key Trends in Business Communications." Report. Accessed September 2, 2014. http://www.heywire.com/downloads/infographics/HeyWireInfographic.pdf.

6 Ibid.

7 Hamilton, Jon. "Think You're Multitasking? Think Again." *National Public Radio*. October 2, 2008. Accessed September 02, 2014. http://www.npr.org/templates/story/story.php?storyId=95256794.

8   State of the Global Workplace. Report. *Gallup*, 2013.

CHAPTER 3

9   Groysberg, Boris. "The Seven Skills You Need to Thrive in the C-Suite." *Harvard Business Review*. Harvard Business Review, 18 Mar. 2014. Web. 10 June 2015.

10 Zenger, Jack, and Joseph Folkman. "Are Different Skills Required For Senior Executives?" *Forbes*. Forbes Magazine, 22 Aug. 2014. Web. 10 June 2015.

11 Wilen-Daugenti, Tracey, Courtney L. Vien, and Caroline Molina-Ray. *Women Lead: Career Perspectives from Workplace Leaders*. New York: Peter Lang, 2013. Print.

12 State of St. Louis Workforce 2013. Rep. Workforce Solutions Group. Accessed June 11, 2015. www.stlcc.edu/Workforce-Solutions/St-Louis-Workforce/Reports/State-of-St-Louis-Workforce-Report-2013.pdf

13 Millennial Branding Student Employment Gap Study. Millennial Branding and Experience Inc., 14 May 2012. Web. 11 June 2015.

14 Boone, Louis E., and David L. Kurtz. *Contemporary Business*. John Wiley & Sons, 2012. 296. Print.

CHAPTER 4

15 Ericsson, K. Anders, Michael J. Prietula, and Edward T. Cokely. "The Making of an Expert." *Harvard Business Review*. Harvard Business Review, 01 July 2007. Web. 07 Aug. 2015.

CHAPTER 5

16 Goldsmith, Marshall. "The Success Delusion." *Marshall Goldsmith Library*. N.p., n.d. Web. 03 June 2016.

17 Folkman, Joseph. "The Best Gift Leaders Can Give: Honest Feedback." *Forbes*. Forbes Magazine, 19 Dec. 2013. Web. 31 Aug. 2015.

CHAPTER 6

18 Gallo, Carmine. "Steve Jobs, Ashton Kutcher, And The 10,000 Hour Rule." *Forbes*. Forbes Magazine, 17 Jan. 2013. Web. 07 Aug. 2015.

19 Ericsson, K. Anders, Michael J. Prietula, and Edward T. Cokely. "The Making of an Expert." *Harvard Business Review*. Harvard Business Review, 01 July 2007. Web. 07 Aug. 2015.

20 Ericsson, K. Anders, Michael J. Prietula, and Edward T. Cokely. "The Making of an Expert." *Harvard Business Review*. Harvard Business Review, 01 July 2007. Web. 07 Aug. 2015.

21 Ericsson, K. Anders, Michael J. Prietula, and Edward T. Cokely. "The Making of an Expert." *Harvard Business Review*. Harvard Business Review, 01 July 2007. Web. 07 Aug. 2015.

22 Heilbroner, Robert. "The Worldly Philosophers." Cliffs Notes. Accessed August 31, 2015. www.cliffsnotes.com/literature/w/the-worldly-philosophers/about-the-worldly-philosophers.

CHAPTER 7

23 "Dominican Research Cited in Forbes Article." Dominican University of California. Accessed August 27, 2015. www.dominican.edu/dominicannews/dominican-research-cited-in-forbes-article.

24 "Dominican Research Cited in Forbes Article." Dominican University of California. Accessed August 27, 2015. www.dominican.edu/dominicannews/dominican-research-cited-in-forbes-article.

CHAPTER 8

25 Tjan, Anthony K. "How Leaders Become Self-Aware." *Harvard Business Review*. Harvard Business Review, 19 July 2012. Web. 17 Sept. 2015.

26 Cashman, Kevin. "Return On Self-Awareness: Research Validates The Bottom Line Of Leadership Development." *Forbes*. Forbes Magazine, 17 Mar. 2014. Web. 17 Sept. 2015.

CHAPTER 9

27 Johnson, Tory. "The Art of Being Barbara." Success.com. Success Magazine, 11 Feb. 2013. Web. 4 Dec. 2015.

28 Freifeld, Lorri. "8 Pillars of Trust." *Training Magazine*. Training Magazine, 21 Nov. 2011. Web. 05 Jan. 2016.

29 Freifeld, Lorri. "8 Pillars of Trust." *Training Magazine*. Training Magazine, 21 Nov. 2011. Web. 05 Jan. 2016.

30 Horsager, David. "Trust As Currency." *Fast Company*. Fast Company, 20 Nov. 2012. Web. 06 Jan. 2016.

31 Chapman, Alan. "Mehrabian's Communication Research." BusinessBalls.com. N.p., n.d. Web. 21 Dec. 2015.

CHAPTER 10

32 "Reputation Under Pressure." *IHHP*. Institute for Health and Human Potential, n.d. Web. 19 Jan. 2016.

33 Freifeld, Lorri. "8 Pillars of Trust." *Training Magazine*. Training Magazine, 21 Nov. 2011. Web. 05 Jan. 2016.

34 Hardy, Darren. "Building Your Personal Brand (Pt 1 of 2)." Darren Hardy. Darren Hardy, 21 Aug. 2012. Web. 19 Jan. 2016.

35 Taibi, Catherine. "The 16 Best Things Warren Buffett Has Ever Said." *The Huffington Post*. TheHuffingtonPost.com, 30 Aug. 2013. Web. 21 Jan. 2016.

36 Sullivan, Gail. "Puppy-kicking CEO Forced to Step Down."
    Washington Post. The Washington Post, 3 Sept. 2014. Web. 22 Jan.
    2016.

37 Ronson, Jon. "How One Stupid Tweet Blew Up Justine Sacco's
    Life." *The New York Times.* The New York Times, 14 Feb. 2015.
    Web. 16 Apr. 2015.

38 Ronson, Jon. "How One Stupid Tweet Blew Up Justine Sacco's
    Life." *The New York Times.* The New York Times, 14 Feb. 2015.
    Web. 16 Apr. 2015.

39 Baumeister, Roy, Ellen Bratslavsky, Catrin Finkenauer, and
    Kathleen Vohs. "Bad Is Stronger Than Good." *Review of General
    Psychology.* 5.4 (2001): 323-70. Web. 22 Jan. 2016.

CHAPTER 11

40 Heath, Chip, and Dan Heath. *Made to Stick: Why Some Ideas
    Survive and Others Die.* New York: Random House, 2007. Print.

41 May, Kate Torgovnick. "How to Give More Persuasive
    Presentations: A Q&A with Nancy Duarte." *TED Blog.* TED
    Conferences, LLC, 31 Oct. 2012. Web. 23 Feb. 2016.

CHAPTER 12

42 "Short and Sweet Speeches Lessen Audience Anxiety." Bob
    Schieffer College of Communication. Texas Christian University, 9
    Mar. 2014. Web. 08 Mar. 2016.

43 Gallo, Carmine. "9 Public-Speaking Lessons From The World's
    Greatest TED Talks." *Forbes.* Forbes Magazine, 4 Mar. 2014. Web.
    08 Mar. 2016.

44 Morgan, Nick. "Why Is Passion Important in Public Speaking?"
    Forbes. Forbes Magazine, 23 Dec. 2014. Web. 03 May 2016.

THE POWER OF INFLUENCE

45 Rohn, Jim, and Darren Hardy, perfs. *Lessons of a Lifetime*. Success, 2012. CD.

46 Addison, John A., and John David Mann. *Real Leadership: 9 Simple Practices for Leading and Living with Purpose*. N.p.: McGraw-Hill Education, 2016. Print.

47 Addison, John A., and John David Mann. *Real Leadership: 9 Simple Practices for Leading and Living with Purpose*. N.p.: McGraw-Hill Education, 2016. Print.

INDEX

gestures, 139

goals

accountability partner and,
106–107

leadership and, 38, 161

self-discipline and, 105–106

Goldsmith, Marshall, 77

growing influence

choosing change, 71

commitment, 63–66

motivation for, 72

overview, 61–63

resistance to change, 66–69

self-discipline, 69–71

Growing Your Business (LeBlanc),
22, 90

Groysberg, Boris, 43

H

Hardy, Darren, 27–28, 156

Hatler, Pat, 105–106, 108–109

Heath, Chip, 165

Heath, Dan, 165

Heckler, Lou, 118, 143, 153, 157

Heywire Business

business communication on
personal devices, 18

business-related texting, 16–17

Hildebrandt, Phil, 154, 204

honest feedback

challenges to receiving and giving,
77–79

six steps to, 83–84

trust and, 79–80

Horsager, David, 140, 155

I

IHHP (Institute for Health and
Human Potential), 151

*Illuminate: Ignite Change Through
Speeches, Stories, Ceremonies,
and Symbols* (Duarte), 167

Illusory Superiority phenomenon
(Above Average Effect), 3–4

impact

brevity, 191–193

communicating with passion,
195–196

creating standout experience,
187–189

eye connection, 189–191

Influence3, 185–187

leaving lasting impression, 197

overview, 183–185

pausing, 193–195

In Denial quadrant (Resistance
Matrix), 68

indirect communication, 47–48

Influence Model

adaptability, 54

avoiding getting caught in
internal dialogue, 175–178

knowing audience, 167–169

motivating audience, 165–167

overview, 163–165

preparation, 169–171

reading audience, 172–175

consistency, 53

authenticity and, 137–139

between message and delivery,
53, 137, 141–144

non-verbal communication,
134–137

ABOUT THE AUTHOR

Stacey Hanke's passion is teaching others how to communicate with influence Monday to Monday®. As a keynote speaker and mentor to C-suite executives, she helps individuals see through the eyes and ears of their audiences. The result is career-changing insights.

Over the last twenty-plus years, Stacey has trained thousands of leaders, salespeople, and business professionals across the United States and abroad. The influence skills and techniques she shares build the confidence, credibility, and presence that create lasting results.

Stacey Hanke, Inc., the company she founded in 2004, provides keynotes, training, and coaching for organizations in a wide variety of industries, including manufacturing, healthcare, retail, advertising, financial, and insurance. Stacey's clients encompass Fortune 500 companies and household brands such as Coca-Cola, GE, General Mills, Kohl's, Blue Cross Blue Shield, US Cellular and abbvie, Leo Burnett, and several branches of the US Armed Services.

Stacey has authored articles for BusinessWeek.com and is the co-author of *Yes You Can! Everything You Need from A to Z to Influence Others to Take Action*. Articles about Stacey and her thought leadership have appeared in *The New York Times* and *SmartMoney* magazine. Recognized as one of the National Speakers Association's "Top 6 Under 40," she has emceed TEDx, and has appeared on the Lifetime Network and WGN Chicago.

Stacey attributes her drive and Monday-to-Monday® work ethic to the lessons she learned from her parents, lifelong Midwestern dairy farmers. She now calls Chicago home. A certified fitness instructor, she spends her weekends inspiring others to lead healthy lives.

Follow Stacey at www.staceyhankeinc.com.